The Search for Heaven

Worldwide representation:
Global Lion Intellectual Property Management, Inc.
P.O. Box 669238, Pompano Beach, FL 33066
Phone: 754.222.6948. Email: charlie@globallionmgt.com
Website: http://www.globallionmanagement.com/

The
Search
for
Heaven

*A Historian Investigates the
Case for the Afterlife*

Dr. Jean-Pierre Isbouts

Bestselling Author of National Geographic's
The Biblical World

PRAISE FOR BOOKS BY JEAN-PIERRE ISBOUTS

National Geographic's The Biblical World: An Illustrated Atlas

"The National Geographic Society, under the editorship of Professor Isbouts and a team of advisors, has produced a visually stunning atlas of the Bible .... The historical spectrum runs from the dawn of civilization and the traditions of Genesis through the biblical history and on into the spread of Christianity and the beginnings of Islam. The quality of the historical commentary for each period matches that of the illustrations."
—Dianne Bergant, The Bible in Review

"For its scope, beauty, and relevance in today's world, this unparalleled atlas has become a classic." *—Booklist*

"Isbouts writes in a nondenominational style that allows non-expert readers to follow along easily. The atlas's more than 50 stunningly detailed color maps from the National Geographic Society contain notations that place the regions, cities, mountains, and rivers in context of the events discussed.
–Jennifer Jack, American University Libraries.

"A visually stunning atlas of the Bible." *—Donald Senior, C.P., The Bible in Review*

National Geographic's Who's Who in the Bible

"Isbouts has written an exquisite reference guide to the personalities in the Bible. This well-researched and well-organized work will complement what is already on your shelf."
—Jacqueline Parascandola, Columbia University Libraries

"Occasionally, a book will arrive that is so impressive in

its presentation that I stop immediately to look through it. Such is the case with Who's Who In The Bible: Unforgettable People and Timeless Stories from Genesis to Revelation by Jean-Pierre Isbouts ... The scholarship is deep and without the usual presuppositions."—*John D. Pierce, Baptists Today*

"Dr. Jean-Pierre Isbouts is brilliant and did a magnificent job in his research and writing of this book. This surpasses any biblical reference book I have on my shelves. I enjoyed being transported to biblical times while reading and viewing the photographs in this masterpiece. A must-have for any biblical scholar, student, professor or layman."—*Ordinary Servant*

National Geographic's In the Footsteps of Jesus

"Dr. Jean-Pierre Isbouts has written widely on the genesis of Judaism, Christianity and Islam... I was moved by his text challenging me more deeply to follow the Way, Truth, and Life. I felt that I was following Jesus again."—*Carol Ann Morrow, St. Anthony Messenger*

"What emerges from the book's pages is a very modern portrait of a grassroots spiritual reformer, fired by the socio-economic injustices of the Galilee and Judea of his day. This makes the book surprisingly relevant for our own era, when the Middle East is once again convulsed by the collision of political, religious and ideological forces."—*Santa Barbara Independent*

"This detailed nondenominational account will capture history lovers and the faithful alike and provide important historical context for the life of Jesus and the rise of Christianity."
—*War Cry*

"The book reconstructs the historical, social and cultural conditions of Jesus' time by exploring the people, places and politics of the world in which he lived... "In the Footsteps of Jesus" is an ambitious undertaking led by Jean-Pierre

Isbouts, a humanities scholar and professor at Fielding Graduate University in Santa Barbara, CA."—*Kim Shippey, Christian Science Sentinel*

From Moses to Muhammad

"An exciting and scrupulously fair book, in a field where excitement often overwhelms fairness. Not here: Isbouts is a trustworthy guide throughout a perennial minefield." – *Francis E. Peters, Prof. Emeritus, New York University*

"With sweeping narrative and vivid analysis, Jean-Pierre Isbouts shows that Judaism, Christianity, and Islam are rooted in common sources of revelation." – *Prof. Bruce Chilton, author of "Rabbi Jesus"*

"Jean-Pierre Isbouts makes a most important contribution to help overcome negative stereotypes." –*Rabbi David Rosen, Director, Interreligious Affairs, American Jewish Committee*

Ten Prayers that Changed the World

"As a history teacher myself, I was immediately drawn in by Isbouts' storytelling. Vivid descriptions coupled with historical context provided a greater depth and understanding of these accounts."–*AnAnchoredFaith.com*

"Isbouts places the reader right in the thick of the action." –*Rebecca Hitt, "Stories in My Pocket"*

"Isbouts has a storyteller's gift..." –*Tonya Parham, "Books Make Everything Better"*

"Jean-Pierre does an impressive job of looking at each story through a purely historical viewpoint, not crossing over into theology and a potential minefield. A good reminder of how one person really can change the world and how God sometimes uses the most unlikely of characters to do so." –*The Christian Backpager*

Young Leonardo: The Evolution of a Revolutionary Artist

"*Young Leonardo* offers a highly original and exceptional insight into the gestation of Leonardo da Vinci as the leading artist of the High Renaissance." –*Dr. Bernard Luskin,*
Chancellor, Ventura County Community College District

"This satisfying book ... (shows) how Leonardo's career was forcefully shaped by the politics and intrigue of the period." –*Richard Cytowic, New York Journal of Books*

"*Young Leonardo* offers a wonderful journey into the wellspring of Leonardo's creativity and the incredible path to his achievements. A brilliant story well told. –*Dr. Frederick Steier, University of South Florida, Tampa*

"In this meticulously researched and visually rich book, Jean-Pierre Isbouts and Christopher Heath Brown unravel an historical mystery – and come up with surprising results that will surely change our understanding of the evolution of Leonardo's most iconic work." –*Dr. Rich Appelbaum, Distinguished Research Professor, University of California at Santa Barbara*

Contributors

Sue Dunderdale Jones
Internationally renowned British psychic

Kimberly Cantergiani
Jennifer Decker
Andriana Eliadis
Michelle Elias
Audrey Ordenes
Laura Sherwood

Doctoral students in the Social Sciences PhD program of Fielding Graduate University of Santa Barbara, CA.

TABLE OF CONTENTS

The Lagoon Nebula, located 4,000 light years from earth, is a massive stellar nursery that vividly illustrates the universe's infinite cycle of destruction and rebirth (*source: NASA/ESA*).

Introduction

*"If you look into your own heart, and you find
nothing wrong there, what is there to worry about?
What is there to fear?"*
Confucius, ca 500 B.C.E.

Let me begin by asking you a question. When was the last time
you thought about dying? Or the afterlife, for that matter? You
don't remember?

You're probably not the only one. We are far too busy to think
about unpleasant topics like that. Our daily lives are consumed by
things that we believe are much more important: our daily chores
at work, at home, at school, at the gym or the grocery store, or
trying to get the kids to music or soccer practice on time. Is it any
surprise, then, that we rarely have a moment to ourselves? And
that, even if we do, our first urge is to look for our smartphone and
see who's been texting or posting in the last five minutes? There
isn't enough time in the day, so why would anyone want to think
about something as depressing as dying? We've got other things
to worry about.

Of course, if we are honest with ourselves, the reason we don't
want to think about death is because it *terrifies* us. The idea that
all the wonderful things that we surround ourselves with will one

day come to an end is simply too terrible to contemplate. Much better, then, to ban it from our thoughts, this whole end-of-life business, and to live our life in happy denial.

Until it hits.

And when it does, when a loved one—a parent, say, or a spouse or close sibling—actually dies, we are devastated. We are overcome with grief. Because we are utterly unprepared for that shock. Because we refuse to accept the inevitability of it. Because we believe it is *not fair*. Or as Lili Tomlin put it recently in a CNN TV show, "Death is a drag. You come into the world and you have to die at the end? I'm like, who thought this up?"[1]

For most of us, the idea that we could have another identity, a *spiritual* identity that may just survive our physical self, doesn't really enter into the equation. Why not? Because we no longer believe that we have a soul, or a spirit, or anything else along those lines. Yes, we may listen to sermons about heaven or paradise at our place of worship, but deep down inside, we no longer believe it could exist. As rational human beings, we have given up on that idea.

And that's not entirely our fault. For over a century now, scholars and scientists have been telling us that it's all a mistake; that at the end of the day we are simply made of carbon, and *only* of carbon. I know, because I was once one of them. As a scholar, I found it very difficult to accept that some unseen part of us could somehow survive our death. Even our medical profession, all the wonderful physicians and specialists who try to keep us alive, are invested in that same idea: that human beings are mortal. As one researcher recently phrased it, "the prevailing clinical model is that death is an enemy, and that within the medical profession, death is a failure." Therefore, our lives should be sustained as long as possible, and death should be delayed at all costs, no matter how painful or expensive or utterly pointless such efforts ultimately prove to be.

True, there may be Christian or Muslim physicians who privately nurture the hope that a heaven or a Jannah could exist, but if they do, they know to keep such thoughts to themselves. In our modern culture, science and faith do not mix. Therefore, the idea of heaven is not a subject for serious scientific inquiry. End of story.

So why do I now feel differently? What made me change my mind, and launch my decade-long investigation into the scientific evidence of the afterlife? The answer is that throughout my career as a historian and biblical scholar, I've become increasingly intrigued by what other people in history thought about death and the afterlife. And what I found is that surprisingly, people in the past had a much more positive outlook on life. I know that sounds strange, because we all think that today, we stand at the pinnacle of human achievement. The 21st century! The age of robotics and artificial intelligence! That should make us the happiest people in history, should it not?

The answer is, *not really*. The truth is that in some ways, we know *less* today than people did in the past. And the reason, I think, is that life for them was much more precarious than our own. Most people truly lived on a knife's edge of survival. And as a result, they were much closer to their spiritual sense of self.

Let me give you an example from my book *Archaeology of the Bible*. Until the mid-19th century, most folks toiled as subsistence farmers—as families who eked out a living by growing crops that were barely sufficient to see themselves through another season. That made them extremely vulnerable, because drought, famine, floods, wild animals, thieves, or the outbreak of war could wipe out their means of existence in an instant. At the same time, only about half of all newborns, on average, lived to adulthood. One or two out of every five women died in childbirth. Disease, or any illness for that matter, was often a death sentence, for modern medicine did not exist.

And yet, because these people lived on the precipice of death, they were much closer to life. You begin to value your existence very differently if every day is a struggle to see your family fed, clothed, sheltered, and safe from danger. That's why these men and women *sensed* a lot more about the fragility of life than we do today. That also gave them a much more intuitive grasp of their spiritual dimension. For them, the spiritual self was a consolation, a refuge, particularly because the *physical* dimension of their condition was so often fraught with anxiety, pain and suffering.

Compare that to our modern lives today. We have become so attached to the material comforts of our First World existence that it has begun to monopolize us. When we stand in an elevator, or wait in our car before a red light, we whip out our smartphones lest we be left alone with ourselves for just a few seconds. For me, there is nothing more tragic than to see couples, and even families, sit around a table in a restaurant, glued to their cellphones. Unlike the men and women of times past, we have lost the art of being alone with ourselves. And if that's true, then it's no surprise that we dread the end of that comfortable material existence. It also means that because of our overwhelming need for material gratification, finding the spiritual dimension within ourselves has become so much more difficult.

I think that is why, as rational human beings, we no longer ponder the possibility of life beyond death. That's why we meekly accept that all of our knowledge, our consciousness, our love, our hopes and dreams are ultimately destined for the dust heap. Thrown out with the trash! Gone.

You and I may not be aware of it, but we are victims of what modern scholars call *material monism*—the idea that we are nothing but an organic machine. And because this is now the prevailing ideology of our modern age, all of our science is predicated on that reductionist belief as well. Our physics, our social sciences and our medical practice are all rooted in the essential and definitive mortality of human life.

After all, the biological functioning of our anatomy is the only thing that can be observed, digitized, encoded, and put under a microscope. Therefore, we think that biology must be the only thing that matters. For example, neuroscience has now progressed to a point where we believe we can pinpoint individual behaviors in specific areas of the brain. Neuroscientists therefore assume that human consciousness must be *synonymous* with neuronal activity. In other words, our mind is nothing more than our brain, and if you take that away, there is nothing left.

But this is the question that kept me awake at night: if our modern science is correct, then why is it that every other period in human civilization believed something entirely different? Why is it that from the very beginning, people always thought that they did not have a single but a *dual* dimension: an existence based on mind and matter, on body and spirit? Go to any point in history— whether the ancient Egyptians, Sumerians, Persians, Chinese,

Indians, Mayas, Incas, or Native Americans—and you'll find that all of these peoples arrived independently at the same conclusion: that even though we may die, some essence of ourselves continues to exist. The Greek philosopher Plato called it the "spark of the divine;" the soul (*psyche*) that animates us as human beings from birth. According to Plato, the body merely serves as a vessel before the soul can return to its pure state of being.[2]

So why have we lost that innate sense of mind and matter, of having both a physical and spiritual self? Is it because in our modern day, we have rigorously banned such ideas to the realm of religion, outside of rational thought? Have we become so cynical about our existence that we think we are no better than the things we surround ourselves with: stuff with an expiration date?

That is the essential question that I wanted to investigate.

For example: read any scientific journal on the question of human consciousness and it will argue that all consciousness is simply a function of brain matter, of little grey cells in your head. Take that away, these scientists say, and you're left with nothing. That argument reminds me of Plato's wonderful story of the cave. In case you're not familiar with it, the story goes something like this: a bunch of people have been imprisoned in a cave, and here they have lived all of their lives, chained to the wall. The only thing they see are shadows projected on that wall in the front of them. What they *don't* see, however, is that the shadows are actually caused by lots of people passing in front of a fire, outside their vision. Naturally, over time these unfortunate prisoners come to believe that these shadows *are* the reality, rather than mere reflections of the reality behind them. They give these shadows a meaning that does not actually exist.

Similarly, the scientists who observe our brain believe that this network of neuronal activity *is* our conscious mind, rather than merely the physical manifestation of that mind. But what if these neurons are just the *shadows* of our consciousness? Simply because there appears to be a correlation between our thoughts and the biological activity of our brain doesn't mean that the two are one and the same.

The problem is, our modern science is largely an empirical practice based on observation. That means that despite the high level of our scientific knowledge, we can only perceive what our human faculties enable us to perceive. And therein lies the danger, because we are loath to accept that there may be limits to that perception, and to our ability to understand the world around us. In other words, our science has become so all-knowing that if there is something that science cannot explain, then clearly it cannot exist. It is the nature of the beast—we don't like to accept that we can be wrong.

But no matter how technologically advanced our science may be, we don't know *everything*. We may know more than what previous generations knew, but there is plenty that still eludes our grasp.

CHANCES ARE, IF YOU ARE INTERESTED in the possibility of an afterlife, you've probably read one or two books on the subject. Among others, you may have read Eben Alexander's wonderful *Proof of Heaven*.[3] So what, you may ask, makes this book different? What can I tell you that you don't already know?

My answer is that most books on the market today focus on the afterlife *from a single perspective*. People who have gone through a Near-Death Experience (NDE) talk about that experience. Psychics who have been in touch with spirits talk about those visions. Psychologists and hypnotherapists who have used regressive therapy talk about their case studies. Christian, Jewish or Muslim authors naturally look at the afterlife through the unique prism of their faith. Meanwhile, historians focus strictly on ancient concepts of the afterlife without comparing these to modern ideas. And few, if any, of these authors have dared to grapple with exciting new discoveries about immortality in fields like astrophysics and quantum mechanics.

In sum, there is a whole mountain of new data from all kinds of research, but no one has ever attempted to put all of this evidence together, in order to try to build a practical model of the afterlife. Or answer questions like, *why* does it exist? How does it function? And *why* does it function the way it does?

We can't help it: we are a society of specialists. In my career, I have often observed how scholars and practitioners are deeply uncomfortable with stepping outside the familiar boundaries of their field. But without that, we will never be able to see the big picture.

My aim in this book is to do exactly that: to make my case by presenting evidence from a vast range of sources, just as a prosecutor will sway a skeptical jury with the overwhelming testimony from different eye-witnesses. In doing so, I feel a bit like Colin Wilson, who wrote that the evidence for the afterlife is so immense that "it is like standing at the foot of Mount Everest and insisting that you cannot see a mountain."[4] But until now, no one had actually tried to climb that mountain, and gather all the evidence along the way.

The Stories of this Book

So how will we go about it? First, I will take you to the beautiful island of Bali. Here, we will experience first-hand how everything that the Balinese do is governed by their spiritual agency.

Based on those impressions, we will then try to understand that spiritual agency by looking through the prism of modern science—for example, by looking at electromagnetic energy. We will find that almost all of the great discoveries of the 20th and 21st century have to do with *energy*, from the biggest phenomenon— Einstein's general theory of relativity—to the smallest: quantum physics.

Our next foray will take us into the strange world of NDE's, of Near Death Experiences, as well as regressive hypnotherapy (RHT). We will look at scores of case studies that cut across age, gender, language, religion, socio-economic status, and cultural background. In psychological studies, these variables usually determine very different outcomes. But in the case of near-death or regressive experiences, we will find that none of these factors play a role whatsoever, and that a Muslim man in Iran can have the same postmortem experience as that of a Christian woman in the United States.

Equipped with that knowledge, we will then plunge into the experimental world of neurology and quantum physics, to try to understand this thing called "human consciousness." We will explore the wondrous world of our brain as visualized through modern fMRI techniques, and discover how much quantum philosophy has in common with the idea of humans as spiritual beings.

Next, I will introduce you to an even more incredible domain, the psychic world of my collaborator, the famous British psychic Sue Dunderdale Jones. Together, we will witness some truly astounding events that cannot be explained by conventional science, as further evidence of the remarkable power of spiritual energy.

And then we will reach the high point of our adventure: a journey through the spiritual universe, based on all of the evidence we have compiled to date. This is the "mother ship" from which we came, and to which we will return. I know that sounds a bit like science fiction, but believe me: based on everything we will have learned at this point, this journey will seem entirely plausible, filled with the most incredible visions you've ever seen.

After we arrive back on earth, I will next take you through the ideas of heaven as articulated by our religions, and ask the question: do these models agree with what we've just seen? To what extent is our idea of Paradise, Heaven, Jannah, She'ol, or Nirvana in sync with the spiritual universe that we have just visited? And what does that mean for our beliefs? This is an area where many people get a bit nervous, but rest assured: there is nothing here that will upset you as a believer. On the contrary: as a practicing Christian, I find tremendous joy in the fact that the evidence in this book confirms much of what the Bible tells us.

Lastly, this book will address the question, what does it all mean? What does it mean, Alfie? This is the question that I ask my doctoral students when they struggle to finish their dissertations, because without fail, that is the one thing they tend to overlook. But isn't that the essential purpose of science? To have a practical 'take-away'? To make a positive impact on the quality of our lives?

Well, here is my purpose in writing this book. Simply put, it is *to dispel your fear of death*. I know that seems like a tall order. All of us live in fear of death. And the reason is that it is programmed in our biology. As organic creatures living on earth, we have been predicated on *survival* since the dawn of time, and anything that stands in the way of that goal is a threat. That explains this deep, innate fear of death, because death will seemingly defeat the essential purpose of why we think we have been put on earth to begin with.

But that is a fallacy. Our purpose on earth is not to prolong our mortal life as much as possible—on the contrary. The reason why our spiritual identity took on a human form, and why it will just as easily shed that human coil, is because of the experiences we will have, the decisions we make for ourselves and those around us, and the meaning we extract from that experience. I know that may sound strange, but I am confident that at the end of this book, you will know what I am talking about.

What this also means is that heaven is *meant for all of us*. It is not a reward for the righteous; it is not an exclusive club reserved for the elect. It is part of the way we are programmed from conception and birth. It is, quite simply, embedded in our DNA. And if that is true, then we should be able to find evidence for that process in modern physics. That is my essential argument, and the thread of the logic that we are going to follow in this book.

Imagine, then, the joy of living our lives to the fullest, knowing that death is *not* the end. That beyond the threshold of dying lies another, even more wonderful world: a world without pain or suffering, without violence or hate, without prejudice or social divisions, where everyone is equal under the warm embrace of a supremely intelligent agency.

Could such a utopia really exist? Could there really be such *premeditation* in the universe? As the evidence in this book will show, I believe the answer is yes. Everything we do and experience in our lives is ultimately the outflow of a loving energy that sent us out on our mission, and that will call us back when our time has come.

Knowing that death is *not* the end can fill us with a new sense of purpose, but it can also radically change the way we grieve for the death of others. I was devastated by the death of my mother, now four years ago, but my research for this book has convinced me that I will see her again at some point in the future, and that she—and other loved ones who have gone before me—will be waiting to embrace me once more.

Knowing that death is not the end may also change the debate about euthanasia and other forms of assisted death, and make patient choices very difficult to ignore. And finally, it would also change the religious dimension of that debate, because we would recognize that the ability to move to the joy of life after death is simply part of God's plan. So if, after reading this book, your apprehension about our inevitable death is less, then I have met my purpose. And perhaps this knowledge may help you to live a more loving and meaningful life.

Jean-Pierre Isbouts

The Pura Taman Saraswati temple in Ubud, Bali, is dedicated to
Sarasvati, the Hindu god of learning, art and literature.

1. A Voyage to Bali

So what is this thing called our "spiritual dimension?" That's a difficult question, because it's not something that we can readily see. It's not something that you can touch, feel or smell. It simply *is*. Over the centuries, many folks have come up with all sorts of names for it, such as 'soul' or 'spirit'. Greek philosophers like Socrates and Aristotle use the term *psyche*, which, literally translated, means "life-breath."

These Greek sages argued that this strange, ephemeral *psyche* is actually the very core, the very essence of ourselves; our inner engine. That which gives us our identity, a sense of *self* in the truest meaning of the word. Of course, we should remember that life in ancient times was not a walk in the park. As we saw in the previous chapter, for most people life was a daily struggle. But they also saw and experienced things that we can no longer see. Imagine, for one moment, what it would be like to spend each evening under a sky filled with stars as bright as diamonds. For most of us, that is no longer possible. Our cities produce so much illumination at night that we no longer know the majesty of a pristine night. Just the other day, *The New York Times* printed a color image of our galaxy, the Milky Way, strewn across a night sky, as photographed from one of the most desolate places on earth. The author wrote that in our modern day, most of us will never see this incredible image with our own eyes. But before the

Industrial Revolution, this was a commonplace sight for most of humanity. Perhaps that explains why all of the three Abrahamaic faiths—Judaism, Christianity and Islam—originated in the desert.

Another thing that ancient civilizations knew and cherished was the idea of a holy place—a very special spot where spiritual energy seemed to flow in abundance. Over the years, as part of my wanderings as a public speaker, my wife Cathie and I have been very fortunate to travel to such places. One of these is the Greek sanctuary of Delphi, nestled in the grey limestone of the Parnassus Massif. Another is the Inca citadel of Machu Picchu, located high up in the Andes Mountains, in the heart of Peru. But nothing prepared us for the intense experience of visiting the island of Bali.

What is it that makes Bali so special? Of course, like all visitors we fell in love with its emerald-green rice terraces, its deep river gorges and pristine beaches, which are populated by some of the most beautiful people on earth. But what really struck us was this palpable sense of spirituality that emanates from thousands of shrines and temples, both large and small, from every village on the island.

In fact, Bali is in many ways a time capsule from bygone times. While much of South East Asia was upstaged by the Islamic conquest, European colonial rule, and the violent upheaval of 20th century politics, Bali remained mostly untouched because of its isolated location. Save for a brief period of oppressive Dutch rule, the Balinese were left alone to live their lives the way their ancestors had done for centuries.

As a result, visiting Bali is like stepping in a time machine to travel back thousands of years—that is, if you're willing to leave the splashy resorts on the south coast to venture deep into Bali's heartland. What you will find is a place of ancestral beliefs that have all but disappeared from the rest of the world. Think of it as the spiritual equivalent of the Galapagos Islands—an incubator of an ancient culture that, by rights, should no longer exist. And yet, against all odds, it still does.

Naturally, Bali has not been totally immune from outside influences. Hinduism, for example, sunk roots here around the time of the birth of Christ. But under the surface of Hindu worship lives a far stronger and more ancient Balinese tradition that goes back thousands of years: the cult of *animism*. As the word implies, animism (from the Latin *anima*, meaning "breath" or "spirit") is the belief that the physical world around us is governed by unseen entities called *spirits*. Some of these spirits can be benign, in which case they are revered as gods; but others are thought to be evil, and those are feared as demons.

Animism is one of the world's oldest religious traditions. It assumes that everything around us is possessed by a spiritual quality—not only living things like animals, but also flowers, plants, trees, even rivers or rocks. These are powers that our five senses—sight, sound, taste, touch and smell—cannot perceive, but for the Balinese they are a tangible reality. In fact, this ancient belief permeates everything that a Balinese man or woman does. They accept that spirits can sometimes become demons if they are not treated with respect, with grave consequences for themselves and their families. Therefore, all Balinese are taught from an early age to keep both good and evil spirits in balance, in much the same way that Chinese philosophy sees the world as the product of the opposite forces of yin and yang. Just as fire and water coexist, so too does light and dark, but in Bali this dualism cannot be taken for granted. It must be managed, abetted, and assuaged on a daily basis. The result is an elaborate liturgy of rituals that every Balinese, both young and old, adheres to scrupulously.

For example, I once saw a young girl reach down to pick a flower. But before she did, she said a prayer for its spirit. You see that same reverence in all of the island's temples, carvings, paintings, and even its dances. It is the task of every Balinese to keep these spirits in balance, and thus secure the harmony between man and woman, young and old, human and divine. The Balinese have a word for it: *sekala niskala*, which means "visible (and) invisible."

That also reveals another side of Bali: its social cohesion. Assuaging the gods is not something an individual can do. It literally takes a village in which everyone is asked to participate. One day, for example, we drove across the island to visit a temple that is devoted to the most important essence of Balinese life: water. Water is a holy substance, because without it, life could not exist. In fact, the Balinese believe that water increases in sanctity the closer you get to its source. That is why this temple, called Pura Tirta Empul, was built near the source of its sacred spring (*pura* means temple; *tirta* means water; *tirta empul* means "holy well").

As we entered the temple, we expected to see a quiet sanctuary filled with whispering worshippers. To our surprise, what we saw was a forecourt with a huge *petirtaan* or "pool" where families splashed each other in crystal-clear water, laughing, playing, and having a good time. They don't perceive their worship as a duty, but as a way to connect with their spouse, children, and greater family.

Walking through a village one day, I noticed that a small box of flowers had been left in the dirt as if abandoned or forgotten. Careful not to step on it, I wondered why anyone could be so careless as to leave this simple offering on the street. But then I discovered that there is a purpose to these gestures, for the lower gods—the *bula kala* or demons who can make life quite difficult—draw their power from the soil. That means that they live low to the ground. That's why their sacrifices are left where they can find them, on the ground, near the threshold of a home or temple—to ensure that the demons don't enter and start to make a fuss. With this token of respect, the Balinese hope that the *kalas* will be mollified, or even become a force of good.

Of course, the good gods dwell on high. That means they need to be invited down to earth so that they can be entertained. As a result, Balinese temples—unlike other Hindu sanctuaries elsewhere—are wide open spaces, punctuated by small pavilions called *bale*. Here are throne-like shrines known as *pelinggih*, where the gods are invited to sit. Colorful parasols are sometimes added to these shrines, to shield the god from the sun.

You would think that all this pressure to maintain the forces of the universe would be a source of stress for the Balinese, but the opposite is the case. I have seldom seen people so happy in their environment, despite (or perhaps because of) the very modest scope of their worldly possessions. That's because most Balinese draw their happiness from the natural bounty in which they live: the abundant fertility of the rice fields; the lushness of the rainforest; and the incredible profusion of birds and wildflowers that surround them. And knowing that the spirits will protect and guide them gives the Balinese a sense of security that is all but lost in our modern civilization.

Animism in Other Worlds

But how primitive is animism, really? Is it truly as alien as we might think? Just open up the text of any Gospel, and you will see that the world of Jesus was just as permeated by spirits and demons as that of the Balinese today. To give you one example: immediately after Jesus declared the start of his ministry in a synagogue in Galilee, he was confronted by a man possessed by an "evil spirit." Jesus rebuked the spirit, and the congregation was amazed, saying, "He commands even the unclean spirits, and they obey him."[5] Later that evening, long lines began to form at the house of Peter's mother-in-law in Capernaum, where Jesus was staying. His fame had spread all over Galilee, and people from the nearby villages brought "to him all who were sick or possessed with demons."[6]

What is remarkable about these stories is that Jesus not only appears to recognize these spirits and demons, but actually engages in a discussion with them. In fact, these demons seem to know more about Jesus than everyone else in the story. "Whenever the unclean spirits saw him," Mark writes, "they fell down before him and shouted, 'You are the Son of God!'" (Mark 3:11-13). It is the demons, rather than the people, who recognize that Jesus is divine himself. The Greek word that Mark uses for demon, *daimónion,* has its root in the verb "knowing." Plato uses the term *daimon* to mean "knowledgeable" or "wise," as did other ancient authors. In other words, demons were believed to be intelligent, supernatural beings.

Similar ideas about spirits were also present in Arabia before the advent of Islam. The world of the Arab nomad was inhabited by countless evil spirits or *djinns*, which usually sheltered in wild animals, in trees, or even under a rock. "Whereas the Jews and Christians culled their prophecies from scripture," says one author of the early Islamic period, "the Arab soothsayers received their foreknowledge from the djinns, spirits of the air who supposedly stole information by listening close to heaven." The belief in evil spirits even survived the spread of Islam; the *Hadith* (a collection of sayings by the Prophet Muhammad) says that whereas Adam was formed from matter, and angels were made from light, demons were made from fire.[7] As a result, even to this day some Muslims use amulets to ward off the whispers of evil spirits (*waswas*), lest they penetrate the heart and cause evil thoughts.

Spirits in our Modern World

What are we, in our modern age, to make of all these stories of spirits, good and bad? Do we simply dismiss them as the product of ancient superstition? Or is it possible that ancient peoples may have had a more intuitive grasp of their spiritual dimension than we in our material world?

As we saw at the beginning, we live in an age of supreme reductionist monism. That means that we are so attached to the comforts of our First World prosperity that we cannot conceive of anything that is not material, that we cannot touch, see, hear, or otherwise perceive. It also means that anything that we cannot explain is simply dismissed as irrelevant.

We have hinged our entire existence on reason and rational science, to such a degree that we have lost our ability to sense things beyond the material world. As the philosopher Wayne Jackson put it, "we are now living through a period of history in which people are so blown away by the success of physical science, so moved by the wonders of technology, that they feel strongly inclined to think that the mathematical models of physics capture the whole of reality." But, he continues, that is simply not the job of physics. "Physics is in the business of predicting the behavior of matter, not revealing its intrinsic nature."

So if we remain stuck in our material monism, we're not going to get very far in understanding the mechanics of the afterlife. But the people we just encountered, not only the Balinese but the people of the ancient Near East, believed something entirely different. They realized that there is a spiritual dimension that survives the threshold of death, as we did ourselves before the dawn of the modern age.

Now you're probably thinking, "Is he really expecting us to believe that there are spirits and demons around us, even in our modern world? Are we supposed to think that these spirits can either help us or make our life difficult, as the Balinese do? And if so, where are these spirits coming from? How do we know that they're real? And why would they want to get involved in our lives? What is it to them?"

Yes, I know, these ideas are difficult to accept. After all, if there are spirits in our lives, why can't they make themselves known to us? Why can't they tell you where your car keys are, or the glasses that you've been looking for all day? Wouldn't that be your first response? If there are these spirits, why don't they make themselves *useful*?

We can't help it—we are products of the age of reason, where everything must have a practical purpose. But what would you say if I told you that these spirits *have* been trying to make themselves known to us? That they have been doing that since our birth, but that we are too dim-witted to sense it? Is it possible that we have lost some sixth sense, some innate intuition of our spiritual presence, which was so obvious for people living in a simpler age?

The answer to these questions may simply be a matter of semantics. Words like "spirits" and "demons" are things we intuitively associate with superstitious beliefs, with primitive religions, or with Hollywood fantasy movies. But what if we called them something else? What if, instead of spirits, we referred to it as *energy*?

Now, that is something most of us can get our head around. We all understand energy, or at least, we *think* we understand it. Even though it is something that we cannot see, we are still prepared to accept it as a quantitative reality in our lives. For example, when you buy a picture with a magnet that sticks to your refrigerator door, you are confident that when you get home, some unseen power will pull it towards the door and keep it there. You can't *see* that magnetic energy, but you have no problem believing that it exists, and that it will keep your magnet snugly attached to your refrigerator. Similarly, you know that when you hold an apple in your hand and let it go, the pull of gravity will drop it down to earth. You cannot see gravity, but just like Newton, you accept that it exists. What these examples show is that even in our material world there are things, such as energy, that we cannot see but that we do accept. And that is the key point that we will make in this book: that when it comes to understanding energy, we are babes in the woods. We have yet to truly grasp the extent to which various energies govern our lives.

In fact, it is not an exaggeration to say that almost all of the great discoveries of our modern age have to do with our dawning understanding of energy: from the biggest—Einstein's general theory of relativity—to the smallest: quantum physics. Put simply, without energy we could not exist. Even our own bodies produce quantitative energy—the equivalent of about 80 watts— by processing carbohydrates and proteins with oxygen. When we are under stress, or run a few miles, that output can even increase to some 1,000 watts! Similarly, the earth itself, with its seasons, climates and ecosystems, is driven by the radiant energy from the sun and the geothermal energy from its inner core. Not to mention, of course, all the trappings of our mechanized technology, which depends on the energy produced by fossil fuels or renewable sources such as solar and wind power.

In fact, much of what we always thought of as static, physical matter is actually a quantum of energy. Quantum physics have revealed that there is no such thing as static matter, and that all things are simply atoms in motion. It's the speed of the atoms that makes the difference.[8]

The problem is, as humans we cannot *see* or in any other way sense these energy sources; we can merely study their effect. So here is something that should give us pause: we think we know it all, but we don't. While we have many wonderful senses, our bodies are not equipped to perceive what is probably the most important element in nature: its sources of energy. I would even go so far as to predict that this century and the next will see many more groundbreaking discoveries about the role of energy, and that these revelations will radically alter the way we think about ourselves and our role in the universe.

Back in the early 1930's, one of the most celebrated British physicists was a man named Arthur Eddington. Among others, he was the first scientist to confirm Einstein's theory of relativity, and later was the first to posit that the most important source of energy in the universe is actually nuclear fusion.[9] You would expect such a man to be deeply wedded to the material certainties of his science, but Eddington surprised everyone by declaring that we don't really understand the physical world. What we see, he said, are merely its outward manifestations, like the shadows in Plato's story of the cave. Eddington used the metaphor of a bundle of threads. We're only pulling at threads, he said, and yet we think we know what's behind it, in much the same way that a paleontologist may try to reconstruct a dinosaur based on a fossilized footprint.

Such a startling admission from so prominent a scientist, is rather revealing. Eddington went even further, and suggested that there is some form of continuous dimension, some universal source of energy, that directly connects with our inner consciousness. In fact, he said, this energy field governs and informs all elements of the universe—including us as human beings.

Until recently, such ideas were an absolute anathema in the academic community. If you wanted to hang on to your tenure as a professor, you were well advised to stay clear of such ideas, for they smacked of parapsychology, or worse, occultism. But just in the last few years, some scientists have begun to accept that our current understanding of physics cannot explain the whole story. In fact, the more we learn about the physical make-up of the universe, the more we realize what we *don't* know, and what still needs to be discovered.

One example is the recent suggestion that there must be some unknown form of energy, called *dark energy,* that makes up as much as 68% of universal density. Scientists such as Stephen Hawking have argued that this mysterious force is the reason why the expansion of the universe appears to be accelerating. But just in the last few years, scientists have come around to a different view. Rather than calling it "dark energy," which sounds like some destructive force from a science fiction movie, they are beginning to recognize that this may actually be driving the whole show. And so they have given it a new name: the *quintessence.* In other words, many physicists are ready to accept that although we cannot see what is perhaps the most powerful source of energy in our universe, it may very well be the force that shapes it in the first place.

Here's another example of the power of energy that may be a little closer to home. If you're like me, a man in my early 60's, you've probably had an MRI scan done at one point in your life. MRI technology uses Magnetic Resonance Imaging to visualize and diagnose human pathology, and these images can be quite amazing. But what you may not know is that just in the last decade, a number of scientific papers have reported that this magnetic energy can sometimes produce behavioral changes that no one can explain. In one case study, the energy from an MRI significantly improved the mood of bipolar patients.[10] In other cases, patients suffering from rheumatoid arthritis were surprised to experience a substantial improvement.[11] Additional studies have shown that magnetic resonance can even have a significant impact on alleviating pain in other diseases.[12] A number of new studies are now underway to determine if electromagnetic radiation can be used as a curative tool, particularly in bone and nerve regeneration, as well as in cancer therapy.

My point is this: we have become so blind-sighted by our obsession with physical matter, and the progress of our medical technology, that we ignore the fact that other forces are at play in our lives—not only in nature but in the universe as a whole. As Philip Goff notes in his book *Consciousness and Fundamental Reality*, our view that the world is fundamentally physical in nature is deeply flawed. It may explain the extrinsic, mathematical features of material properties, but it fails to understand their intrinsic nature, or why they exist in the first place.[13]

Goff's conclusion is that the famous British philosopher Bertrand Russell was right: that there must be a *panpsychism*, some form of energy or consciousness that pervades all living things, down to particles, atoms, cells—and even quantum waves. The renowned Danish physicist Niels Bohr meant the same thing when he declared that "the electromagnetic field acts like it is guided by one organized thought." Or as Goff put it: "Is the universe a conscious mind?"[14]

I know this all sounds like stuff that is "far out," as we used to say in the 70's. But I hope that at this point, you are ready to accept that the physical world is not all there is. That there are powerful sources of energy that directly influence our universe as well as life on this planet. Let me give you another example.

One day my friend Sue Dunderdale Jones, a British psychic, took a trip to Scotland. She had never visited this region before and had heard from others how beautiful it is. She rented a car and was driving along a country road, enjoying the view, when she suddenly experienced an intense desire to pull over. As soon as she did, she felt as if something was nudging her to walk to a nearby hill. She obeyed this feeling and climbed across the ridge to find herself in a beautiful, sunlit valley she had never seen before. And then, while standing there, she began to experience intense visions of medieval battle. She saw blood being spilled, limbs being cut off, men dying in vast numbers. The most frightening thing, she later told me, was the sound: the bloodthirsty screams, the cries of the dying, the clash of swords on metal shields. Weeks later, having researched the matter, she discovered that she had experienced a battle that had been fought many centuries ago. The violence that day had been so intense that the valley's energy field had never recovered; its trauma still lingered after 600 years.

I realize that some of you may find this difficult to believe. Indeed, some scholars have dismissed such reports as simply the spontaneous product of a person's subconscious memory. But Sue had never read or heard anything about that battle before.

So what does this mean? One thing is that we may be closer to the Balinese world of spirits and demons than we thought. For if our physical world is held together by another, fundamental reality—such as the harmonics of energy—then that would not come as a surprise to the average Balinese villager. After all, he might say, "and you think this is news? My man, we've known and practiced that for thousands of years!"

The sun is the most important source of energy for life on earth,
by converting 4 million tons of matter into energy *per second*.

2. The Energy Within Us

So let's for the moment accept that the world around us is *not* solely made of physical matter. Let's agree that our environment may, to some extent, be governed by a source of energy that we cannot detect with our senses, but that we know may well exist. If that's true, then it is not a major leap of faith to think that our bodies are likewise dependent on energies that we may not be aware of. For example, when we feel refreshed after a good night's sleep, we say we are "full of energy." By contrast, when we haven't slept well, or have lived through a tough day at work, we feel as if our inner energy is depleted. The same is true when we've come down with a cold, or feel ill; we often say in those situations that we "have no energy at all."

So how do we uncover the secret of this mysterious source of energy? As it happened, our thinking about energy has changed a lot over the past century. First, of course, came Einstein's relativity theory, which argues that the energy of an object is equivalent to its mass, times the square of the speed of light. What that means in plain English is that mass and energy are interconvertible; they are "co-equal properties," as one physicist put it. But that raises an important question: which one comes first? Does mass produce energy, or is it the other way around? Does the tail wag the dog? I know this sounds fairly arcane, but in a sense this discussion is very relevant to the question of whether we as humans have a dual character, one of body and spirit, or simply a monist character—made up of matter only.

Of course, you already know what most scientists would say about the issue. They believe that matter is the primary substance. But that conflicts with quantum theory, which posits that at the end of the day, every substance is a form of compressed energy. If we follow their line of thinking, it is *energy* that runs the show in the universe. And of all the forms of energy that exist in the world, electromagnetic energy is particularly relevant for our story.

About the Sun

What is electro-magnetic energy? One way to answer that question is, when was the last time you went to the beach? After you popped your umbrella and figured out how to open your beach chair, what did you do? You turned the chair in the direction of the sun, sat down, and went, *Ahhhhh*. Right? And why is that? Because the rays of the sun felt good on your face. It felt good all over your body, that warmth, which is why we all like to hang out on the beach. It makes us feel *alive*. And there is a good reason for that. Without the sun in the sky, you and I wouldn't be alive at all. In fact, none of the organisms on earth would be alive.

Without the sun as our primary source of energy, earth would just be another rock in the universe, covered with ice. That same energy also warms the oceans, the continents, and the air in our atmosphere, thus producing our weather patterns. The sun creates the photosynthesis that allows plants and other organisms to produce carbohydrates that serve as our food, and oxygen to enable us to breathe. And when natural sunlight touches our skin, its UV rays trigger the production of Vitamin D, one of the key ingredients that sustain our health. And last but not least, the sun is our primary light bulb, our source of light during the day.

All of these emissions—heat, light, and ultraviolet—are forms of electromagnetic energy. These typically travel in waves, which allows us to determine their wavelength. Radar, radio, television, microwave ovens, X-ray machines and multispectral cameras are all modern applications of electromagnetic energy. In fact, this energy is considered one of the fundamental ingredients in our universe, because it is the only type of wave that can travel through empty space.

That doesn't mean, of course, that all of these waves are benign. If it weren't for the ozone layer around earth, we would be exposed to the harmful effects of excessive ultraviolet radiation. To put that in numbers, the ozone layer, which is found at an altitude of between 12 and 19 miles above earth, absorbs as much as 99% of the sun's medium-frequency ultraviolet light. That is why the erosion of that ozone layer due to the emission of industrial chemicals (such as clorofluorocarbons or CFCs) is so troubling, for stronger radiation would cause skin cancer, the suppression of our immune system, and other potentially lethal damage.

The point of my story is that the world around us is alive with energy—all sorts of energy. Some of these energy waves we can sense, such as light and heat, and some we can't, such as radio, X-ray and ultraviolet emissions. But they are out there, surrounding us on a daily basis, whether we are aware of it or not.

So if that is the case—that our natural world is governed by all sorts of electromagnetic energy—then it may not be a stretch of the imagination to say that our bodies are sustained by some form of electromagnetic energy as well. In fact, just as many of the intangible, non-material elements in nature are animated by energy, the same may be true for things in our body that are not directly related to our organic functioning: things such as happiness, love, or contentment. Think of the joy we experience when we see a beautiful painting, or hear a melody that stirs our heart. None of these things, which are so fundamental to our life as human beings, can be explained as purely material processes. But all of these sensations can lift our spirit in a way that no physical impulse can.

Of course, this is nothing new that I am telling you. Thousands of years ago, ancient cultures had already discovered how important this inner source of energy is for our happiness and wellbeing. They even went as far as to say that the more we were in touch with this inner source, the happier we would be. Conversely, if we ignored that inner energy and simply focused on material gratification, we would inevitably become dissatisfied, possibly depressed, and even physically ill.

Virtually every ancient culture I know of developed some form of practice around this idea, to ensure that humans could function as balanced, holistic beings. The most beautiful of these philosophies is undoubtedly the Indian Chakra tradition. Some 2,000 years ago, Indian gurus discovered a continuous flow of energy in the human body that they believed moves through circuits known as *nadis*. They called this energy *prana*, which means "life force." They also found that because this energy flow is so closely aligned with our body's physical functions, its purpose is not only to keep us physically healthy but also to stabilize our behavior, our thinking, our emotions, our consciousness. In the words of Laura Sherwood, chakras form the bridge between the two dimensions of our being: the physical body (*sthula sarira*) that is made of matter, and the "subtle body" (*suksma sarira*) that consists of our consciousness, our mind and our emotions.

In sum, these mysterious energies try to maintain the harmony between our physical and spiritual being. To do so, this life force operates from a number of key centers in our body, known as chakra centers, which slowly develop through infancy and childhood.[16] A leading Western Chakra theorist, Anodea Judith, believes that the first chakra, located at the base of the spine, unfolds during the first year of life. As we would imagine, this chakra controls our most elementary survival needs, including sleep, eating, or bonding with our primary caregivers. This also stimulates feelings of love and trust, so that in later adolescence and adulthood, this energy source becomes the primary seat of love and the need for attachment. At the same time, it will continue to harbor instinctive functions related to our survival, such as the "fight or flight" response that we will discuss in a moment. As a result, this first chakra is often called the "root" chakra.

After the first year, or as soon as the first chakra is sufficiently mature, the second chakra emerges in the lower abdomen. This is when the child begins to appreciate the feelings of physical and emotional pleasure, and starts to crave the loving embrace, the gentle touch or soothing words of its caregiver. As soon as it discovers its senses of sight, sound, smell, taste and touch, it wants to move about to better explore its world—which is the signal to the parents to "child-proof" their home. Many years later, in adolescence, this is where the body's sexual organs, including the testicles and the ovaries, will develop, thus instilling the seeds of sexual response.

Somewhere between 18 months and four years, the third chakra will begin to unfold. This is when the child develops its self-awareness and autonomy, which will form the foundation for its sense of purpose in later years. Not surprisingly, these are the years that parents often refer to as the "terrible twos and threes," as toddlers try to see how far they can push back against parental authority (and as the father of four, I vividly remember those years!) But of course, this push for boundaries is essential for the child to establish its sense of will, vitality, and initiative in adulthood. As always, this chakra has a physical corollary as well. It is believed to be near the navel, close to the spinal column, so as to better control digestion and the metabolic conversion of food into energy—the essential ingredient of physical strength.

The fourth chakra is located near the heart, and is therefore assumed to be responsible for the roots of human compassion and a sense of social responsibility. It is believed to blossom between the ages of 7 and 12, and endow the child with a growing understanding of its role in the home, the family, as well as the school and community where it lives. In adulthood, this chakra will be the seat of a person's ability to become a productive member in the workplace, to develop team building skills, and to build meaningful relationships with lovers and friends. Some chakra theorists associate this center with the thymus, which controls the body's immune system.

The fifth chakra develops in tandem with the fourth, and is seated near the throat. As the location suggests, this energy center is the source of human creativity. This is when the child begins to discover the power of speech, of communication and learning, but also of its self-consciousness. According to Judith, this center lays the foundation for personal transcendence, key to its future spiritual growth.

Of course, as you already have noticed, the higher we go into the human body, the more elevated the functions of the chakra become. That is also true of the sixth chakra, which is located in the forehead. Some yogis refer to it as the "third-eye chakra." It is associated with the pineal gland, which produces melatonin, and therefore represents light, harmony, and the process of sleep and awakening. As such, it becomes the individual's seat of wisdom, imagination, and higher reasoning.

The seventh chakra is believed to operate from the crown of the skull, and as you probably surmised, this energy center is the cockpit of our physical and spiritual wellbeing. It is the control center that governs all other energy flows, and is often depicted as a lotus flower with a thousand petals. It is also the center of our spiritual essence, of our ability to pray and meditate.

Naturally, this particular chakra energy can only develop if the child's home has some spiritual resonance as well. As a result, I cannot help but think that it is very important for young kids to be raised with the rites and practices of a spiritual tradition, whatever that tradition may be, even if in later years that child will turn its back on religious practices. I know it is hard when that happens; some of my grandchildren have been baptized, whereas others are not. But I believe that there comes a time in the life of every human being when problems become so overwhelming , and only a spiritual response can provide effective guidance. Knowing the path back to a chapel, a synagogue, or mosque will then become very meaningful.

The Evidence for the Energy Flow

Is the Chakra system an accurate reflection of the energy flow in our body? Its practitioners certainly believe so, though the Chakra philosophy itself has many different variations and traditions. Some believe there are only five, or as many as eight chakras; others posit that there could be countless more. The point is that from a very early age, as early as 1000 B.C.E.—the Vedic traditions are as old as ancient Judaism—human beings became convinced that the organic matter of our bodies is utterly dependent on a powerful inner source of energy.

India was not alone in that belief, of course. The 4,000-year-old Chinese practice of *Qigong* argues something very similar. It also believes that our body is governed by the flow of *Qi* or "life energy," which moves through meridians in our body. The Japanese philosophy of *Ki* says much of the same thing. As a result, these theories have served as the foundation of Asian health practice for thousands of years. It assumes that when a person is ill, the flow of energy is out of balance. It is then up to the practitioner to correct this energy flow in the troubled areas of the body. In India, this took the form of Ayurvedic remedies, yoga, and meditation. In China, this prompted interventions such as acupuncture, medicinal herbal remedies, and energy practices such as Tai-Chi.[16]

But the concept of life energy is not limited to Asian traditions alone. In 2016, G. Cajete published a study that found that indigenous peoples of the Americas have similar long-standing traditions, and use it as the wellspring of "knowledge and truth gained from the interaction of the body, mind, soul, and spirit with all aspects of nature." Ironically, Cajete adds, this perspective is not unlike our modern concept of quantum physics, which sees nature as a "dynamic, ever-flowing river of creation and systems of energy."[17]

Most scientists today reject such ideas. While they admit that electromagnetic energy exists, for them it is simply a matter of electrons. But others have begun to take a closer look. The reason, I think, is that quantum physics has upended many of our 20th century certainties, even though we still don't know what quantum physics really mean, as we will see in a later chapter. If it is true that everything that appears as matter is actually atoms in continuous motion, then perhaps we shouldn't so readily dismiss the idea of energy as the principal agent of our human body. Of course, the trick is to prove that this is the case. As children of the Age of Reason, we want to see *evidence*, before we can believe.

That desire has led to the birth of a new discipline called biophysics. Its aim is simple: to determine if there is an all-encompassing energy field that coordinates and regulates all of the primary functions of our body.[18]

Remember the story of the little Balinese girl, who said a prayer for the flower before she plucked it from the ground? She may have been on to something. Back in 1935, two scholars at Yale University, Burr and Northrop, made an astonishing discovery. They were able to detect distinct bio-electric levels in a variety of organisms, including plants. Based on this data, they argued that organisms on earth have distinct "energy fields" that not only control their development, but also their health and even their mood.[19] In the 1970s, A. S. Pressman confirmed these findings by showing that many organisms have "exquisitely sensitive antennae" that can interact with these electromagnetic fields in nature.[20]

In the last few decades, a growing number of physicists have becgun to study this concept. This has prompted the National Library of Medicine—an organization not known for its interest in paranormal phenomena—to include "biofield science" as an official search term, thus allowing scholars to pursue this field without fear of being ridiculed by their peers.

And what have these researchers found? A lot, actually, which puts paid to the notion that the functioning of our body is strictly the business of "genes, proteins encoded by genes, and molecules synthesized by proteins," as our physicians are taught in medical school. [21]

For example, two Polish scientists, Sedlack and Inyushin, found that bioenergy may actually be a form of plasma—an ionized gaseous substance of tremendous electrical conductivity—given that plasma is one of the most abundant forms in the universe.[22] The physicist Walter Kilner went a step further and argued that we should think of the human biofield as an aura. He even tried to photograph this human aura, using different colored screens and filters.[23]

The next step was taken at the University of California Los Angeles (UCLA), where Dr. Valerie Hunt developed a Bioenergy Field Monitoring System (BFMS) that actually indentified a human energy field at 200KHz. In 2015, the physicist M. Mincolla confirmed Hunt's findings with an even more sensitive instrument, which indicated that the entire human body generates an ambient biofield of 0.025 volts of current per centimeter.

It was only a matter of time before these rather radical ideas moved into actual clinical practice. Today, many clinicians and biofield practitioners, including my friend Dr. Rick Levy, are able to *see* a patient's aura, or "biofield" as they call it, and use it to establish a diagnosis. Some believe that this aura is composed of seven layers, whereby the inner layers represent the physical and emotional functioning of the body, while the outer layers (extending two to three feet from the body), serve to establish harmony with the surrounding world. [24]

I know it sounds fanciful, but if that is true, then each of us is surrounded by a luminous field of energy that not only controls our body, but also extends from that body to connect with our immediate environment. It is, in the words of my doctoral student Udall DeOleo, "a vital energy that is a continuous whole, flowing around us in lower and higher frequencies."[25]

Another way to think of it is as an electric current, which permeates our entire being.[26] In fact, that's how the lie detector, a famous device in spy novels and movies, is supposed to determine the truth: by measuring changes in the electric current of the skin and the heart.

But what does this life energy do, exactly? And why is it so important to our story? The answer, I believe, is that it appears to manage all the critical functions in our body on a daily basis.[27] For example, did you know that the cells lining your stomach are replaced every five days? Similarly, your skin cells are regenerated every two or three weeks, while red blood cells are replaced every four months. When you consider that the human body has about 10 trillion individual cells, that means that on average, an adult's body is fully regenerated every eleven to fifteen years. Even more amazing is the fact that all dying cells and organisms emit a radiation that is up to 1,000 times stronger than their stationary emission during homeostasis. Perhaps that can serve as evidence of this mysterious source of life energy.

But managing the operation of our physical functioning is not the only thing it does. At the core of all biofield models lies this fundamental idea of the human body as an essential duality: as a combination of physical matter on the one hand, and "subtle" or "spirit" energy on the other. What that means is that in order to stay healthy we must not only tend to our biological organs, but also to the life force, the *prana* that animates and rules these organs. We must be "mindful," as yoga practitioners tell us. What that means is that you and I can have far greater control over our health than we think. These biofield energies are not abstract essences; they are, to a great extent, responsive to what our mind directs them to do.

Now, that is as far removed from our Western way of thinking as you can possibly imagine. When we have a headache, feel nauseous, or catch a cold, we rush to swallow a pill. If we think we might have contracted a disease of some sort, we run to the doctor, and surrender ourselves completely to the specialized world of modern medicine, of which most of us understand very little. In other words, we no longer believe we have any control over our own bodies. We have abdicated that responsibility to the pharmaceutical industry and the medical establishment, and of course these institutions have prospered as a result of it. Even the most intelligent and strong-willed alpha person is bound to wilt when confronted with the intimidating system of modern medical diagnostics.

Here, again, we should realize that the very developed state of our modern society has actually impoverished us. We have become so dependent on Western medicine that we no longer believe we have any say in what happens to our bodies. But as 4,000 years of Asian medicine shows us, that's not really true. There are several ways in which we can begin to take back some of that control. By doing that, we not only gain a greater command over our physical health, but we also become much more aware of the spiritual part of who we are.

Alternative Health Practices

One way of restoring a healthy energy flow is through acupuncture. Acupuncture refers to the use of inserting tiny steel needles at key meridians in our body to stimulate or alleviate any stagnation or blockage in the energy flow. What this means in a medical sense is that acupuncture stimulates key nerves under our skin that interact with both our mind and our brain to produce certain biochemical responses, such as decreasing inflammatory proteins, or producing more neural hormones. Fifteen years ago, when Dr. Levy and I produced the TV series *Miraculous Health,* acupuncture was still a fairly unknown phenomenon. Today, it is a growing alternative to Western medicine, particularly in the treatment of chronic pain.

As I am writing this, I am receiving weekly acupuncture therapy for a chronic sinusitis condition that my doctors have been unable to cure with traditional Western techniques—including a heavy regimen of antibiotics, combined with sinus surgery. When I asked my ENT (Ear, Nose and Throat) specialists about acupuncture, they were embarrassed to confess that they had not read anything about this practice nor any other form of alternative intervention.

Their academic training had stayed well clear of the topic. This is typical of how most physicians—and particularly specialists—in the United States think about Asian medicine, even though acupuncture is now the fastest growing alternative practice in the country. In a 2002 survey by the National Institutes of Health (NIH), 4.1% of respondents said that they used acupuncture as complementary therapy. Most of these respondents were Asian females living in the West or Northeast of the country.[28] Since then, acupuncture has seen a 32% increase in visits. A more recent study, conducted in 2015 with over 27,000 respondents, showed that the percentage of people using acupuncture as part of their wellness program had increased to 6.7%.[29]

This is quite astonishing, given that most medical insurance programs in the U.S. do not cover the cost of alternative medicine such as acupuncture, or only to a limited extent. What's more, whereas the "early adopters" back in the 2000's were of mostly Asian origin, that distinction had evaporated in the 2015 study. What is also interesting is that according to the latest survey, patients chose acupuncture not only for traditional indications such as lower back pain or muscular pain, but also for hypertension, stress, anxiety, and depression. This clearly demonstrates the efficacy of acupuncture for not only pathological issues but also for the health and wellbeing of our mind.

All of this, of course, flies in the face of what traditional practitioners tell us. The mostly hostile entry on Wikipedia, for example, claims that there is "little evidence of acupuncture's effectiveness," and that whatever benefits have been reported are simply "due to the placebo effect."[30] That doesn't explain why 6.7% of the American population –the putative equivalent of 12.7 million people—are now actively using acupuncture, or why according to Cancer Research UK, acupuncture is now being used effectively for the reduction of vomiting and nausea among British patients receiving chemotherapy.[31]

The Power of Meditation

Another very powerful way to take command of your mind and body, which doesn't cost anything and requires no needles or any other form of intervention, is meditation. What is meditation, you ask? You could probably pose the question to ten different yoga trainers and get ten different answers. The reason is that we are only now beginning to understand how important meditation is to maintain the harmonics of our body and mind.

One definition, advanced by a group of psychologists who use meditation as part of their therapy, is that it "describe(s) practices that self-regulate the body and mind, thereby affecting mental events by engaging a specific attentional set."[32] If you don't find that description very helpful, you're not the only one. Or how about this one: meditation is "a family of self-regulation practices that focus on training attention and awareness in order to bring mental processes under greater voluntary control and thereby foster general mental well-being."[33] Mind you, both of these definitions appeared in the *Journal of the American Psychological Association*, so they carry some authority. However, neither does a particularly good job of describing what meditation is.

So here is my definition: *meditation is a group of techniques that aim to calm the restless human mind, so that you become more fully aware of your physical and spiritual self.* It may not win any APA awards, that definition, but it sure works for me.

And the reason why meditation works is that we live very hectic lives. We are so distracted by all sorts of things that we are no longer aware of what is happening in our body *until it is too late*: until we get a headache, or an upset stomach, or a more serious sign of illness. Mind-body practitioners like Dr. Levy refer to this as dis-ease; in other words, if we don't tend to the physical and spiritual operations of our body, its harmonics will drift out of balance and eventually produce harmful symptoms.

The most frequent cause of this dis-ease is stress. Compared to just a few decades ago, we live under tremendous pressure from day to day, largely because the information flow we must process has grown exponentially. I still fondly remember the time, just a few decades ago, when we used to conduct business with a phone call, a letter, or perhaps a fax or telex. There was a distinct pace to our work day, measured by the time it took for a letter, fax or telex to reach us. What's more, work only began when we walked into our office in the morning, and it firmly ended when we closed the door, punched our card, and headed for home. That pace gave us time to reflect on other things that require our attention, and to find a proper balance between our work life, our family life, and our personal life.

But that era is long gone. Today, we are besieged by a constant stream of data from our smartphones, iPads and laptops, day and night, without let-up. It probably sounded like a great idea to Steve Jobs when he created the iPhone, but the problem is that human beings aren't built to process this data flow on a 24-hour basis. Worse, this constant barrage has made many of us dependent, to the extent that we will compulsively check our email, our texts, or our social media posts all day long. We think we are good at that; we think that we are marvelous multi-taskers, people who can juggle many things at once, but studies have shown that this is a complete fallacy. We are, on average, much less productive than we were just twenty years ago, because our attention is constantly being pulled in many different directions. As a result, we often struggle to concentrate on a single task, because we are always distracted by incoming data that, in most cases, is entirely superfluous and irrelevant to our task at hand. But we cannot help it; we are addicted to the ping of an email or incoming text, just as a gambler is addicted to pulling the handle of a slot-machine: you never know when you'll strike gold.

The result is an epidemic of stress-related diseases in many First World nations, which is good news for the pharmaceutical industry: Prozac, Zoloft, Lexapro and Paxil are just a few examples of the billion-dollar anti-anxiety and anti-depressant industry. Many of these are selective serotonin reuptake inhibitors, or SSRIs, but they have serious side effects. Most prominent among these is the danger that your mind may become dependent on it. Long term, these SSRIs may actually lessen your resistance to stress, thus plunging you in a downward spiral of ever greater medication dosages.

There is good news, however, and that is that stress isn't a unique phenomenon of our time. Anxiety and fear have always been part of the human experience, though in ancient times it wasn't channeled through the iPhone. Back then, human beings were entirely dependent on the harvest or their flock for their survival, and both could easily be destroyed. As a result, the ancient shepherd or farmer had to cope with an environment that was entirely unpredictable. Whether there was a pasture at the end of his month-long trek with his flock, or whether the seeds he'd planted would actually mature to fully grown crops, was not something he had much control over. In each case, it was quite literally a leap of faith.

To mitigate that risk, these people tried to get in touch with the forces that they believed *did* control these events. That is why, in almost every ancient civilization, the earliest gods were all associated with some form of domestication or cultivation: sun, light, water, rain, fire, fertility, creation. For example, in Mesopotamia Baal was the lord of rain and dew; Enki served as the god of fresh water, and Inanna was the goddess of fertility and love. The challenge, of course, was to figure out how to get in touch with these deities. How to assuage them? How to plead with them?

This is how humans came up with the idea of making a sacrifice, grounded in the ancient practice of bartering. Long before there was any form of currency, people traded with one another by bartering goods: here, I give you five barrels of beer, you give me ten bushels of wheat. This is actually the text of one of the earliest written documents, recorded some 5,000 years ago on a clay tablet from Sumer. Naturally, people tried to do the same with their gods: I offer you something that is dear to me, so that you can reciprocate by answering my plea in return.

In both Mesopotamia and ancient Egypt, rites of sacrifice became a key part of official worship, and that practice remained valid through the Persian, Greek, and Roman eras. Ancient Jewish worship, too, revolved around animal sacrifice, which took place on the altar before the great Temple in Jerusalem. Even today, a sacrifice—albeit a symbolic one—still forms part of the Christian Mass, in the form of the Eucharist.

But soon, another way to intervene with the gods emerged, and that was *prayer*: the idea of directly communicating with the unseen forces of the universe. We can see that process in Genesis, the first book of Hebrew Scripture. In the beginning, sacrifice is the dominant form of intervention. The sons of Adam and Eve, Cain and Abel—each representing the agricultural versus the pastoral lifestyle of Bronze Age peoples—decide to bring an offering to God. Cain sacrificed the "fruit of the ground," whereas Abel decided to offer the "firstlings of his flock" (Genesis 4:3-4). That practice continues in the story of Noah, where after the safe return of the Ark, Noah "built an altar to the Lord" and used it to offer "burnt offerings" of "every clean animal and of every clean bird" (Genesis 8:20).

It is only much later in the Genesis story, after a king named Abimelech takes Abraham's wife Sarah as his mistress, that the Bible suddenly introduces the idea of prayer (*tefillah*). God turns to the king in a dream and tells him: "Now return the man's wife, for he is a prophet, and *he will pray for you* and you will live" (Genesis 20:7; my italics). Later on, Abraham fulfilled this promise by praying to God, and "God healed Abimelech, his wife and his female slaves so they could have children again" (Genesis 20:17).

The important thing of this story is that there is no mention of a sacrifice, or any other sort of material *quid pro quo*. Instead, it is the promise of a prayer that persuades the king to let Sarah return to her husband. And from that point on, prayer–or meditative contemplation–becomes the primary venue in the Bible for seeking an intercession by God. The same is true for many other civilizations. One of the earliest sculptures from ancient Sumer, today's Iraq, are so-called *orants* that show men and women with clasped hands in a posture of prayerful meditation. It gave people the ability to use their own spiritual agency to connect with the greater forces of the universe. And through that agency, worshippers could begin to experience a very special bond—not only with God, but also with the spiritual dimension in themselves.

That is how the idea of the essential duality of human beings was born. It would remain a bedrock of thought for thousands of years—until the advent of our modern industrial age. We no longer have to fear that our harvest may be destroyed, because all we need to do is walk down to the local Whole Foods' store and buy the fruits and vegetables we need. We no longer have to worry about the weather, for all it takes is to Google the forecast on our smartphone. And we no longer have to fear the possibility of invading tribes, except, perhaps, in the form of traffic jams on our highways. In sum, the comforts of our First World lifestyle have obviated the existential needs that drove us to spiritual agency in times past.

So when we do find ourselves praying, it is usually in times of great and urgent need: for example, when a loved one has a medical emergency, when we've lost our job, or when we face a gut-wrenching decision that we feel powerless to make. On these occasions, we suddenly feel as adrift and rudderless as the shepherds and harvesters of the past. But for many of us, trying to make that spiritual connection is difficult. Like everything else, prayer is a practice, like a language you must learn in order to become fluent. And if you have not used that particular language for a long time, it may be difficult to find the right words.

The same is true with meditation. In a sense, meditation is not that different from prayer. It allows you to disengage from your physical presence in order to activate your inner spirit, and to "dial in" to the spiritual world around you.

One of the great leaders of the meditation movement in the United States is Dr. Herbert Benson of Harvard Medical School, whom I met some years ago while directing the TV series *Miraculous Health*. For Dr. Benson, the greatest threat to human health is not cancer, but stress, precisely because it has become so pandemic with the growth of the information age. "Stress comes about by any situation that requires change," he notes. "Any change in behavior, whether in your personal life or your work life, carries the potential for stress. A sudden change in your financial condition, a change in your work life, or a change in your marriage can be a deeply disruptive experience."

As it happens, the human body is prepared for moments of intense stress. Psychologists refer to it as the "fight or flight" response. From the earliest of times, humans could suddenly be confronted with a great and imminent threat: an enemy, for example, or a wild animal, or some natural disaster. At such moments, the amygdala in our brain prompts our adrenal glands to produce an instant burst of adrenalin, to help us make a split-second decision: should we run, or should we stand and fight? That mechanism, however, is designed to be used sparingly, at moments of great peril.

What is happening in our modern world, however, is that stress is becoming a constant condition. Fretting about our job, our relationships, our finances or our health is something that our fight or flight response cannot cope with; we're simply not designed to sustain prolonged periods of intense stress. The result, says Dr. Benson, is our current epidemic of anxiety, high blood pressure, depression, insomnia, heart attacks—even infertility.

What do we do in response? We seek refuge in drugs, and of course the pharmaceutical industry is only too happy to oblige. The problem is that these drugs cannot address the underlying problem: the inability of our body to cope with intolerably high levels of stress for a long period of time. It merely blunts some of the symptoms, at least for a while.

"And the inevitable result," says Dr. James Gordon, Director of the Center for Mind-Body Medicine, "is that you feel helpless and hopeless. And you feel that there is nothing I can do. But the funny thing is, only now are we discovering something that traditional cultures have known for thousands of years: we *do* have a way to cope with stress. We *do* have that ability within us. By activating these powers within us. By summoning these great energies within us. And the way to do that is through mediation"— or *mindfulness*, as we like to call it these days. Dr. Benson calls it the relaxation response.

On this topic, at least, many physicians are bound to agree. Transcendental meditation has clinically shown to decrease our heart rate, our metabolism, and our rate of breathing. Brain scans show that meditation also shrinks the amygdala while increasing the hippocampus—thus producing an overall stabilization of our biological system.

However, meditation is something you have to learn, just like everything else in life. It's not difficult, but it does require a commitment: like carving out at least 15 minutes in your daily schedule, and to do it consistently. Some people use their lunch time to meditate in their office, or take time out at home when the kids are off to school. And how do you go about it? Of course, there are many ways to practice meditation, but the one that works for me is the version taught by Dr. Benson.

The Benson Meditation Practice

As he explains it, the challenge of meditation is to learn to disconnect from the millions of thoughts that are going through your mind, so that for a brief and blissful period, you can "unplug" from the world around you. A yoga practitioner I met once described it as a "brief vacation for the mind."

To do that, you must first find a quiet and comfortable place where you are secure in the knowledge that no one will bother you. That means you should also turn off your cell phone and any other distractions that may occur during your meditation session.

That done, sit down in a comfortable pose and close your eyes.

Experienced yoga practitioners may assume any number of lotus positions, but let me assure you, that is not required: simply sitting in a comfortable chair works for many people as well. This is when the hard part begins, because as soon as you close your eyes, you will probably be assaulted by all kinds of random thoughts. It is as if your mind is saying, "Aha! I have your full attention—let's go down the list of all the things we must do today." Of course, the challenge is to *resist* those random thoughts (known as "mind chatter") and to gradually pacify the mind.

To help you do that, Dr. Benson tells his patients to adopt a word, a sound, or a phrase, and to repeat it constantly, so as to "shut out" any thoughts that want to intrude on your session. Practitioners refer to this as a *mantra*, a Sanskrit word based on the root *man* (or "mind") and *trai* ("release"). A mantra is simply a word, or a string of words, that you repeat over and over again in an effort to keep your mind focused. In other words, it is a tool to release the mind from its concentration on worldly things, and allow it to explore the spiritual part of your inner self.

What type of mantra should you choose? Anything you wish, though it's important to remember is that it is not just the words themselves, but also the *vibration* that they engender in your body. A famous mantra is the Sanskrit word *Om* (pronounced "A-u-mmm"), precisely because of the deep vibration that runs all the way down to your pelvis. *Om* means "the beginning and end of all things," and is somewhat similar to "Amen" in its invocation. Experienced yoga practitioners sometimes extend that with a citation from the Yajurveda, one of the four ancient Hindu Vedas, such as *Om Nama Shivaya,* a tribute to Lord Shiva, "the peaceful one."

But of course, a mantra does not have to be Hindu or Buddhist in nature; it can be any word, or a string of words, that have a special meaning for you. When I have trouble sleeping, I use a mantra like *Spirit help me sleep.* You can speak your mantra out loud, or in whispers, or you can simply recite it in your mind—whatever works best for you. The thing to look for is a set of words that are easy to remember and easy to pronounce, and that have a certain rhythm, a *cadence.* The reason is that, as we saw, our human energy fields are full of vibration; therefore, a mantra aspires to establish perfect harmonics between your physical and spiritual wavelengths. Of course, that doesn't happen right away, and like all good things, it requires some practice. But what will eventually happen, as monks in both East and West discovered, is that the sound vibration of your mantra will eventually find its perfect pitch with the vibrations of your inner energy. A yogi once compared it to the way that singing a favorite song, or hearing a beautiful piece of music, can lift you up and make you feel happy all over.

Breathing

Now, to further assist us in "unplugging" from all the thoughts that try to disrupt our relaxation response, we must learn to control our breathing. Breathing is a very important part of meditation, because it has an almost immediate effect on the metabolic operation of our body and its associated energies. The purpose of breathing is, of course, to bring oxygen to our lungs to fire the metabolic process, and to expel the carbon dioxide that is the waste product of that process. But we typically don't manage our breathing very well; on average, we use only about 30% of our breathing capacity. In other words, as a machine, our body doesn't run as well as it should.

To correct that, all we need to do is to start breathing deeper, using the diaphragm and the abdomen, so that we actually intensify our oxygen intake. A typical example is to take 6 seconds to breathe in, and 8 seconds to breathe out. As you breathe out, say your mantra. Do that for a few minutes or so, and you will find that your body begins to relax. It's a very simple stratagem, but it works.

There is one last thing you should do, and that is to consciously relax your muscles. Start with your feet, then slowly work your way up to your calves, your legs, your abdomen, and particularly your shoulders and neck. As you do so, you must *will* these muscle groups to relax. Remember, the purpose of all these exercises is to *relax* the mind: to disengage it from everyday concerns and anxieties, and in the process, to enter a state of reflection and a deep, inner serenity.

The benefits of meditation for our health and wellness are difficult to overstate. Even traditional physicians and practitioners are now acknowledging its health benefits, for it has been clinically shown to reduce stress and anxiety, and has also been used, with some success, in the treatment of depression and addiction.[34] In fact, meditation even seems to have a positive effect on the workplace. Many workers typically report feeling refreshed and rejuvenated after a brief meditation session, which can translate into higher productivity and better creative thinking. In addition, meditation has in some studies been correlated to more positive prosocial emotions and behaviors among people working in groups.[35] That is why, according to the *Financial Times,* a quarter of American companies now offer meditation or other forms of mindfulness practices for their employees in their workplace.[36]

Of course, there are monist scientists who claim that meditation is useful for purely biological reasons. They point to neurological imaging studies that show that meditation involves a shift in brain activity from the right prefrontal cortex, often associated with depression and anxiety, to the anterior cingulate cortex, believed to be the seat of contentment.[37] Others claim that meditation is simply a way to bring about a general relaxation of muscle groups, thus inevitably producing a sense of wellbeing.

That may very well be true, but that doesn't explain why meditation has been associated with spiritual activity for thousands of years. By temporarily "shutting down" our physical awareness, as well as the mind chatter in our brain, we open our consciousness to an entirely different awareness of who we are: our spiritual half. That is why meditative practice is embraced not only by Asian traditions such as Buddhism, Hinduism and Taoism, but also Christian monastic orders, and even some branches of Islam. The great American monk Thomas Keating called the silence of meditation a form of "divine psychotherapy."

Virtually all Asian religions teach that the way to achieve enlightenment is to practice deep meditation. Buddhism, specifically, prescribes meditation as the path to a great inner awakening that can lead us to enlightenment and ultimate nirvana. For Buddhists, the primary purpose of meditation is not to reduce stress, but to gradually disconnect from earthly concerns and desires, for the simple reason that these physical desires are short-lived and will leave us wanting. By contrast, true happiness can only be found in the sense of great inner peace. The fruits of that peace, of that marvelous serenity, says Buddhism, is a wisdom and insight (*Prajñā*) into the true nature of things, which unites our body with the spiritual dimension of the universe. In a sense, that's exactly what Arthur Eddington had in mind when he said that "our minds are not apart from the world," but rather, "glimpses of a reality transcending the narrow limits of our particular consciousness."

Which brings us back to the beginning of this chapter: the idea that the natural world is animated by fields of energy that govern not only the world in which we live, but also energy flows within us. Perhaps that is why the Book of Genesis says that God created man and woman in his own image. Plato said something similar when he argued, some four centuries before the birth of Christianity, that each human being carries within himself a spark of the divine.

For thousands of years, this simple idea of the duality of body and spirit served as the foundation of human civilization, from ancient Egypt to Mesopotamia, from China to Japan, from ancient Greece to Imperial Rome, from the Dark Ages to the Renaissance. It is only in our modern age that we have broken with that fundamental principle. Instead, we are told to seek fulfillment in buying all sorts of stuff, by being hooked on smartphones, and drowning ourselves in the mindless chatter of social media. It has divorced us from our spiritual self, and left us with the rather depressing notion that we are no better than the stuff we surround ourselves with: material goods, to be discarded when they reach their expiration date.

Is that what it's all about?

On the contrary. If anything, I hope that this chapter has persuaded you that *we are not just made of matter.* We are not just a system of physical organs that eventually age, deteriorate, and die. Much as our modern culture and its material reductionism, might want you to think otherwise, the fact remains that we are made of *two* components: body and spirit, matter and energy. That is the essential idea that humankind has always accepted as a basis for our life on earth. So for the rest of this book to make any sense to you, we need to learn to embrace that idea once more.

That said, let's now proceed to the next level of our quest: to see what happens to our body and spirit on the threshold of life and death.

A Greek funerary stela from 350 B.C. shows the deceased, seated, saying goodbye to his wife and child

3. On the Threshold of Life and Death

Death is one of two things: either annihilation and the end of consciousness, or a migration of the soul from this place to another.

Plato

If our human existence on earth has both a physical and transcendental dimension, then the next question must be: what happens to that duality when we die? That our bodies decompose is inevitable; but does our spirit, the very essence of who we are, die as well?

We know how the medical community would respond to that. Sorry, they'd say, but it's lights out. When you die, that's it. *Basta cosí*, as the Italians put it. In fact, just about the only institutions in our modern society who still talk about the afterlife are our religious belief systems, and particularly Christianity and Islam.

Does our soul survive death, as Christian doctrine tells us? But what is our "soul," exactly? Is it our full consciousness, or is it a mere shadow of ourselves, as in the "shades" of Hebrew Scripture? And if so, will that spiritual part of ourselves truly attain immortality?

To answer that question, let's look at what is perhaps the most dramatic evidence of the afterlife: reports of so-called Near-Death

Experiences (NDE), as well as post-death memories produced through regressive hypnotherapy.

Near-Death Experiences

NDE's are experiences in which patients, often suffering from an acutely life-threatening condition (such as a cardiac arrest or coma) were pronounced clinically dead, yet remember crossing into another state of being after they were medically resuscitated. Bruce Greyson, a psychologist, and Jeffrey Long, an oncologist, have described a number of cases where patients could perfectly hear—and sometimes even see—what went on in their hospital room, even though their brain was clinically dead.[38] A 1998 landmark study by Kenneth Ring and Sharon Cooper even documented cases of blind people, including a woman whose optical nerve was irreparably damaged from birth, who was astonished to finally "see" her husband at her bedside during a Near Death Experience (NDE), and witnessed how medical staff desperately tried to revive her.[39]

Studies conducted over the last twenty years have identified more than 5,000 such near-death experiences, not only in North America but around the world. What is so remarkable about these reports is that the pattern of these experiences is surprisingly consistent, regardless of the patient's ethnicity, age, culture, religion, socio-economic status, or language. As I mentioned earlier, in psychological studies these are usually very important variables that account for significant changes in behavior, but in the case of NDE's they don't seem to matter.

The term "near-death experience" was coined by the American psychiatrist Raymond Moody, author of the first major work on

NDE's, a 1975 book entitled *Life After Life*. Moody first became interested in the phenomenon when as an undergraduate at the University of Virginia, he met a psychiatrist named George Ritchie, who told him the following story. When he was 20 years old, Ritchie was clinically dead for nearly nine minutes. But although his brain was dead, his consciousness was not. In fact, Ritchie remembered, he traveled to the afterlife where he saw the most fantastic visions. Moody became fascinated with the subject, and over the course of his career talked to over a thousand patients who had similar experiences. As a result, he wrote, "I must confess to you in all honesty, I have absolutely no doubt, on the basis of what my patients have told me, that they did get a glimpse of the beyond."[40]

According to Bruce Greyson, another notable author and psychiatrist on the subject of NDE's, reports of people who passed the threshold of death and lived to tell about it go back a long time.[41] A number of articles about NDEs were first published in medical journals in the late 19th century, when interest in paranormal phenomena was on the rise. But it is only in recent decades that the topic has gained a large popular following, in part because modern medical technology is now much better equipped to resuscitate people – even those who, by clinical standards, have already passed on. According to one source, at least 65 research studies have been conducted on the NDE phenomenon since Moody's book first came out in 1975, covering nearly 3,500 individual near-death experiences.[42]

For physicians, a person is considered dead when the breathing has stopped, the heart is no longer beating, and brain activity has ceased. But in this chapter, we will hear of some truly astonishing accounts, told by patients who were perfectly lucid and in command of their faculties, even after they had been pronounced clinically dead for several minutes or longer. That evidence—that human beings can be pathologically dead for a long period of time, and yet somehow retain their consciousness—should give medical practitioners pause.

Today there are at least two organizations that try to collect and promote research about near-death experiences. One is the International Association for Near-Death Studies (IANDS), which organizes annual conferences and publishes a peer-reviewed journal called *Journal of Near Death Studies,* available by subscription. Another, open-access resource is a large database of NDE accounts compiled by the Near-Death Experience Research Foundation (NDERF), led by Jeffrey Long, a radiation oncologist. Like Raymond Moody, Long first became interested in the topic through an acquaintance. One day, he was invited to dinner by a friend who wanted to introduce him to his new wife, Sheila. While dinner was served, Sheila told him a truly extraordinary story that we will turn to shortly. Long, who like other physicians was drilled in the belief of the temporal quality of life, was astounded. As he later wrote, "I left the restaurant that night determined to begin my own research on near-death experiences."[43] Several decades later, this has produced a massive on-line database at www.nderf.org, where people from all over the world post their near-death experience, often in fascinating detail. As I am writing this chapter, a new NDE account was posted by a woman from the U.K. just this morning.[44]

This may not be surprising if it is true that, according to a Gallup survey, some 5 percent of the population will have a near-death experience at some point in their lives.[45] A study by Greyson, Holden and James has compiled some 2,500 NDE reports in the United States, as well as 670 such accounts elsewhere in the world, including Asia.[46] Taken together, these testimonials offer what is undoubtedly humankind's first credible window on the passage from life to eternity.

The Pattern of a Near-Death Experience

To give you an idea of what such an experience may be like, I'd like to tell Sheila's story as reported in Long's book *Evidence of the Afterlife,* as well as other related stories that corroborate Sheila's account.

When we first meet Sheila, she is a healthy young woman who has decided to undergo elective surgery, as many modern women do these days. Long does not specify the nature of the surgery, but we can safely assume that it was not life-threatening in any way. Before she underwent the procedure, however, she did warn her surgeon and her anesthesiologist about one important condition: all her life, she had suffered from severe allergies. This was duly noted, but her doctors did not believe that this condition posed a serious threat. And so the surgery was scheduled, Sheila was intubated and anesthetized, and the operation began. All went well until the patient suddenly showed symptoms of major distress. Apparently, she was experiencing a severe allergic reaction to some of the medication she was receiving. Despite frantic efforts by the surgical team to stabilize her, Sheila had an intense cardiac infarction. Her heart stopped, as did her breathing and her brain activity. By the standards of modern medicine, she was dead. Here is what Sheila experienced from that moment on:

"Immediately after my heart stopped I found myself at ceiling level. I could see the EKG machine I was hooked to. The EKG was flatlined, and the doctors and nurses were frantically trying to bring me back to life. The scene below me was a near-panic situation."[47]

The so-called Out-of-Body Experience or OBE is one of the most common first stages of an NDE. What happens is that the conscious self—the part that guides our thoughts and sense of identity—suddenly finds itself separated from the body that has harbored it. For most of us, the idea that our mind could be removed from our physical body fills us with dread. But surprisingly, most NDE patients described it as a seamless and very natural process. Another woman named Diana who experienced an NDE in 2016 described the sensation as follows:

"My next realization was that I was no longer frightened about not being able to breathe on my own. I was at peace and very aware of the steps the doctors and nurses were taking to save my life. I understood all the terms they were using and could comprehend that I was not alive as far as they were concerned. I became aware of the state of each person's relationship with others in the room. There were suddenly no secrets and yet, there was no judgment on my part, but rather an unconditional love. I felt very much loved at

this time and I wanted to extend that to the others
in the room. But they could not hear me."[48]

This report shows is that as soon as her out-of-body experience began, Diana could perceive things that others could not. She suddenly understood all of the medical jargon that the staff was using, even though she had no medical training. More importantly, she felt the intensity of the emotional relationships among the people in the room, including her relatives who were gathered around her bed. "There were suddenly no secrets," Diana wrote, and yet she found herself unable to judge the thoughts and desires of these people, as she had done in life. What she felt, instead, was an unconditional love.

What's more, she was "at peace." This is a sentiment reported by almost all NDE patients. This is how Sheila described it:

> "In contrast to the chaos below, I felt a profound
> sense of peace. I was completely free of any pain."

Freed from their infirm body, NDE patients revel in the sudden release from the pain and suffering that they experienced just moments before. In 74.4 percent of reported NDE cases, this then leads to an overwhelming sense of peace and serenity. One patient described it as a "feeling of belonging, of meaning, of completeness," as if he had finally come home after a long journey.[49]

Many other patients, including Sheila, then moved on to a next stage:

"My consciousness drifted out of the operating room and into a nursing station. I immediately recognized that this was the nursing station on the floor where I had been prior to my surgery. From my vantage point near the ceiling, I saw the nurses bustling about performing their daily duties."

This passage shows that Sheila's conscious entity is no longer tethered to the body in any way, and that it can freely float about and decide to leave the room where doctors and nurses are desperately trying to resuscitate her body. This is often a prelude to what comes next.

"After I watched the nurses for a while, a tunnel opened up. I was drawn to the tunnel. I then passed through the tunnel and became aware of a bright light at the end of the tunnel. I felt peaceful."

Passing through a tunnel towards a bright light is the most frequently cited event in a near-death experience. It marks the moment when Sheila's spiritual entity is being led to a realm that is no longer of this earth, even though she remains fully conscious of what is happening. Arshan, a Shía Muslim from Iran, experienced something very similar in 2015:

"I was flying and entered into a gray-colored environment. I tried to reach a gray and dusty light that was moving in front of me. As I got closer to this light, it became brighter.... I didn't know

what it was. The light didn't bother my eyes and
wasn't blinding. I was pulled towards the light
with great force. The closer I got to it, the more joy
and peace I felt."[50]

This account clearly shows that a Muslim like Arshan can have
the same experience as a Christian like Sheila. Though they may
interpret it differently, the visions and sensations are essentially
identical. What this tells us is that these glimpses of the afterlife
are not determined by their religious orientation. On the contrary:
they appear to be part of the same biological process by which the
spirit removes itself from its host, the body.

What's more, Arshan's comment about the nature of the light
is corroborated by other accounts as well. Many NDE witnesses
struggle to describe the color of the light at the end of the tunnel.
Some describe it as a "bluish light transitioning to white," whereas
Arshan described it as "a vapor or smoke that is lit up under a street
light. It was formless and had colors of blue, orange, yellow, and
gold." What everyone seems to agree on, however, is that while
the light was intense, it was not blinding or painful to look at. One
person spoke of a "pure light... pure as in something you've never
seen before or could ever put in words."

But what is the purpose of this light? Is it a portal, an entryway
to an entirely different domain? Here is how Sheila described the
next stage of her journey:

"After I passed through the tunnel, I found myself
in an area of beautiful, mystical light. In front of
me were several of my beloved relatives who had

previously died. It was a joyous reunion, and we embraced."

This is perhaps the most astonishing phase in Sheila's NDE. At the gateway, she is welcomed by her relatives who have passed before her. This clearly signals that at that point she is no longer in the earthly realm. She has truly entered a new world, a world that is strange and beautiful, and because of that, perhaps unsettling. This may be the reason why many patients report seeing deceased relatives that they know and love, as if these beings are there specifically to assist her in this transition.

For example, one patient described how she was greeted by all the people who had played a major role in her life, and who had gone before her. Sometimes these appearances are purely sensory, in the sense that the individual "felt" the presence of her loved ones; at other times, witnesses heard their voices, though some NDE patients also report "seeing" these relatives as they appeared in life. According to Long's survey, 57.3 percent of all reports involved an encounter with deceased beings, though these beings always involved blood relatives rather than friends or acquaintances.

What virtually all reports agree on, however, is the feeling of being surrounded by a deep sense of love. "I was introduced to family ancestors and people that I had met that had passed over," an Australian man named David wrote, "and I was filled with love and joy that I cannot describe while I was in their presence."[51] A Spanish woman named Marina expressed it as follows:

"I felt peace and tranquility, like an inner and

outer peace, peace, peace and more peace. There was complete and serenity wrapped in a sense of timelessness or eternity. I had the sensation of living there all my life, as if I had always been there."[52]

In fact, Marina continued, "I had no memory at that moment of the identity I now have." It was as if her life on earth had been a mere fleeting instant, and of no account. "I had no memory of what it is to be a human or about anything that comes with it like eating, sleeping, or travelling," she wrote. "I just felt love and ecstasy."

This is the dissolution phase when the individual feels no longer bound by the linear continuum of space and time, as we do on earth. In other words, time no longer matters; what happens can feel like mere moments or years, depending on the quality and intensity of the experience. "I had no sense of time as I know it here on earth," one patient said; "no sense of the serial nature of time.... Past, present and future were all experienced at every moment while I was in the light.[53]

One striking aspect of many NDEs is the lyrical way in which patients describe the intense beauty of the environment in which they found themselves. Diane wrote that "a whole new reality was revealed to me, similar to the physical world, but, in this higher vibration, more colorful, more beautiful, more amazing. I saw plants, trees, mountains, lakes, animals, and shimmering crystal-like buildings." Another patient posted, "the grass, trees, and flowers were all so exquisite that my mind said so and in return, a vibration of love flowed back to me from them."[54]

At this point, some NDE patients enter what is perhaps best described as a "life review." Some see highlights of their life as if it were compiled in a video montage. "I saw every important event that had ever happened in my life," wrote one patient, "from my first birthday to my first kiss to fights with my parents. I saw how selfish I was and how I would give anything to go back and change." A young Spanish woman posted in 2008, "it was amazing how my life was shown with events I had completely forgotten about and others that were so insignificant that it felt like I was seeing each frame of the personal movie of my life on earth. I realized that I understood everything with a great clarity and super-lucidity I had never experienced before... I realized I had wasted time in suffering and what I should have been doing was using my freedom to choose true love, and not pain, in all that came into my life."

Inevitably, many experts have viewed these reports with great skepticism, or have tried to "explain" NDEs as simply the manifestation of psychological or neurological distress. Some believe these experiences are really hallucinations prompted by either depersonalization or disassociation as a result of a post-traumatic stress disorder.[55] Others see its cause in physiological complications, such as the impairment of the brain's frontal lobe functions as a result of restricted blood flow, or the impact of endorphins and other chemicals produced by the brain at the onset of death.[56] Other "explanations" suggest that NDE's are simply the product of poorly administered anesthesia, anoxia (insufficient oxygen), hypoxia (too much oxygen), or other forms of lobe impairment, thus prompting hallucinations. Some experts—and this one is particularly creative –have even gone as far to suggest that the NDE experience is essentially a pre-mortem desire to return to the womb, in which the dying brain recreates the birth passage through a tunnel towards light and warmth.[57]

Each of these claims can be refuted with several counterarguments, but for me, three stand out. The first one is that the majority of patients who reported an NDE were perfectly lucid, and had no prior history of mental illness or any other form of cognitive impairment. Second, I always like to tell the story of a psychotherapist who steadfastly believed in the hallucinogenic source of NDE's—until he, himself, had a near-death experience. As he later wrote, "The experience I had was totally real. It was definitely not anything like a dream, nor was it like the detached feeling you get during a hallucination on LSD, where there is a dream-like quality of watching yourself, but not really being part of what is going on."[58]

But the third and most powerful counterargument is the incredible consistency of the 5,000+ NDEs reported to date, despite major differences in age, gender, education, socio-economic status, or even the severity of the patient's medical condition. This is also true for near-death studies conducted by two Chinese researchers, Zhi-ying and Jian-xun, on survivors of the great 1976 Tangshan earthquake.[59]

To illustrate this striking concurrence, two neuropsychiatrists at the University of Virginia, Nancy Zingrone and Carlos Alvarado, developed an inventory of the most prominent NDE features across three separate studies, conducted between 1983 and 2002. This table, based on the Near-Death Experience Scale (NDE Scale) developed by Greyson in 1983, is shown on the next page.

Features of NDEs Collected Using Greyson's NDE Scale

Elements and Features of the Scale	Greyson 1983	Greyson 2003	Schwaninger et al. 2002
N	74	27	11
Cognitive Elements			
Altered sense of time	64%	18%	9%
Accelerated thought process	19%	44%	9%
Life review	22%	30%	9%
Sudden understanding	30%	30%	18%
Affective Elements			
Feeling of peace	77%	85%	100%
Surrounded with light	43%	70%	63%
Feeling joy	64%	67%	18%
Feeling cosmic unity/oneness	57%	52%	45%
Paranormal Elements			
Out of physical body	53%	70%	90%
Senses more vivid than usual	38%	15%	54%
ESP	23%	11%	0%
Visions of the future	16%	7%	9%
Transcendental Elements			
Another world	58%	63%	54%
Encountered beings	26%	52%	72%
Mystical being	47%	26%	63%
Point of no return	26%	41%	45%

Source: Holden, Greyson and James, *The Handbook of Near-Death Experiences,* 2009.

Even though not all features were present in the majority of NDE's reported, the comparison shows that:

1. Virtually all respondents experienced a sense of peace and calm, in strong contrast to the trauma of their physical condition;
2. A large majority found themselves separated from their body, a phenomenon for which no scientific explanation has ever been found;
3. Most found themselves surrounded by light, in what was clearly "another world," while feeling intense joy.

Inevitably, for all of these patients there came a moment when they realized they were taken back to their mortal existence, usually because their attending physicians were at that point able to resuscitate their body. In some cases, the patient had no control over this—she or he was simply returned to the physical presence. Others, however, were given a *choice*. So it was with Sheila:

> "Do you want to go back?" I was asked. I responded, "I don't know," which was just like my old indecisive self at the time. After further discussion, I knew the choice to return to my physical body was mine. It was a most difficult decision. I was in a realm of overwhelming love. In this realm I knew I was truly home."

The idea that the spiritual realm is the true home of our conscious self, whereas the earthly life is merely a temporary stay, is a common expression of many NDE patients. As a result, many report having struggled with the decision to either remain in the afterlife, or to return to their bodily presence. If they choose to stay, their experience is, of course, never recorded here on earth, though we do also have reports of past-life experiences through regressive hypnotherapy, which we will discuss shortly.

Some patients are not given the option to stay in the spiritual domain, and many of these experience a feeling of intense regret and disappointment when they find themselves living in an infirm body once more. But others do make the decision to return, usually because of a deep obligation they feel towards a spouse, to their children, or to other loved ones. As Sheila wrote:

> "Finally I returned to my body, and woke up in the ICU over a day later. I had tubes and wires all over me. I could not talk about my profound experience."

It was only much later that Sheila summoned the courage to express what had happened to her. Since she was in a Catholic hospital, she decided to share it with one of the nurses, expecting to receive a sympathetic response. But, she said, "the nun responded with a look of shock and fright." You would expect a religious woman to be delighted with such a clear affirmation of the afterlife, but the opposite was true. In response, Sheila felt an "enormous reluctance" to share her experience with anyone else, for fear of being ridiculed.

The reaction to Sheila's story is no exception. Many witnesses say that they kept their experience to themselves, for fear of being mocked as delirious or mentally unstable. That does not change the fact, however, that for these patients their NDE was a life-changing event. Being endowed with the privileged knowledge of what awaits beyond the threshold of death has filled these witnesses not only with a sense of peace and wonder, but also with a joyful anticipation. Imagine, if we could inspire all of humankind with that same sense of confidence and peace—how different our world would be!

Indeed, as we will see in the final chapter, many NDE patients say that the experience inspired them to make their remaining time on earth as meaningful and loving as possible.

Another remarkable aspect of these stories is how these witnesses describe the beings—let's call them *spirits*— around them. One woman named Diane wrote,

> "I saw beings moving about, light beings, going about their daily lives. They don't have physical bodies, but they are distinct fields of energy. They don't walk, they float. They have lives much like ours, but without the struggles and sorrows. They are artists, musicians, dancers, singers, inventors, builders, healers, creators of magical things... things they will manifest in their next lifetime in the physical universe.

The presence of these spirits was the subject of a separate study conducted by Emily Kelly in 2001. Based on an analysis of 74 cases,

Kelly found 129 references of patients encountering spiritual beings. Most of these (81%) were family members who had passed before them, while some also found themselves reunited with a deceased spouse or other individuals from the patient's generation (16%), or in a tragic 2% of cases, their children or nephews. In the majority of these encounters, patients reported being "close, or very close" to the spirits in question.

Kelly also found something else that surprised her: the opportunity of meeting with loved ones was strongly correlated to the patient's cause of death: either a fatal accident or a cardiac arrest. What these two causes have in common is their *abruptness*, their near-instantaneous impact—unlike, say, a chronic illness like cancer, where death is to some extent anticipated over time. This is simply my hypothesis, but it is possible that given the suddenness of a car collision or a heart attack, some mechanism determines that the patient may need the comfort of a loved one to help negotiate the sudden transition into the afterlife.

Afterlife Reports in Regressive Hypnotherapy

In the 1970's, many psychologists became intrigued with the use of hypnosis in the treatment of psychological disorders. While under hypnosis, patients could often articulate underlying causes of their illness, such as disturbing memories or childhood trauma, that their consciousness had long suppressed. The use of hypnosis in the treatment of mental disorders goes back to Victorian times, but as Theodore Barber argued in 1974, hypnosis could only become a valid clinical tool if it was practiced as part of a comprehensive cognitive behavioral therapy (CBT) program under the supervision of qualified psychologists.[60]   One psychologist who was intrigued by the possibilities of hypnotherapeutic intervention was Michael Newton. He was particularly interested in the use of so-called age-regression hypnosis, whereby the therapist gently guides the patient back in time to some of the earliest memories buried in the subconscious.

The distinction between our "conscious" and "subconscious" mind originated with the famous Austrian psychotherapist Sigmund Freud, who argued that our mind operates on several levels. Our conscious mind is the part that operates our normal reasoning facility on a daily basis. Beneath that is another level, the subconscious, which among others serves as a huge vault of our memories from early childhood. Think of our mind as a computer, which has only limited operating memory and can therefore store only a certain amount of data in our instantly available "random-access memory." Thus, things we need to be aware of at any moment in time, for example while driving a car, are available at the conscious level. Thoughts, ideas or experiences that may be important but that are not required for instant retrieval are placed in our subconscious, so as not to draw memory and "processing power" from our consciousness. As the psychologist Pierre Janet wrote, that doesn't mean that our subconscious is in any way less powerful or less important; on the contrary, it is just as significant as our conscious mind, though it manifests itself at different levels, such as in our intuition, our emotions and even in our dreams. Some authors believe that there is a third level, the superconscious or "higher consciousness," which contains our Higher Self, the identity that in Arthur Schopenhauer's words "rises beyond all experience and thus all reason" to directly connect with the universal energy that we spoke of earlier.[61]

I'm going to leave it at that for the moment, because we will explore the mysteries of our consciousness in more detail in the next chapter. What matters is that Newton believed that age-regression hypnotherapy would allow him to uncover things in his patients' subconscious that they themselves might not even be aware of. As he later wrote, he hoped that hypnosis would allow his patients to "connect with their innermost thoughts and feelings."

As Newton's practice of regressive hypnotherapy became more frequent, something extraordinary happened. He found that several patients didn't stop at their recollections as a very young child. They went back *even farther*, past the moment of their birth, and found themselves reliving their stay in a spiritual universe, a domain inhabited by spirits, *before* being born on earth. At first Newton thought that these memories were simply fantasies, or the product of the patient's spiritual or religious beliefs. But then he discovered that while some of his patients— both men and women—were indeed deeply religious, others were not, and in fact practiced no form of spirituality at all. What's more, the nature of these patient testimonies about their time in a spiritual universe were strikingly similar.

As a result, Newton began to accept that these testimonies represented something very significant that had nothing to do with a patient's imagination. As he wrote, these reports offered "a set of past experiences that were too real and connected to be ignored."[62] It also made him realize that if these observations were indeed authentic, they would allow him to see something that no one had ever experienced: to "see into the spirit world through the mind's eye of a hypnotized subject, who could report back to me of life *between* lives on Earth."

To give you one example: one day, Newton accepted a patient who came to him complaining of chronic pain in his right side. Newton brought the patient into deep hypnosis, and led him in an age-regression exercise. To his surprise, the patient revealed that he had served in the French armed forces during World War I, and that he had been killed by a German soldier plunging a bayonet in his side. Having recognized the source of his chronic affliction, Newton wrote, "we were able to eliminate the pain altogether."

Newton's thesis has far-reaching consequences, because it implies that we as humans will experience reincarnation—the idea that after death, we will at one point be sent back to earth to be born once more as an entirely different persona. For many people, that idea is very difficult to accept. Reincarnation or "transmigration" is a key tenet of Asian religions such as Hinduism and Buddhism, as well as Hasidic Judaism, which believes in gilgul or the transmigration of souls as described in the Kabbalah. But as we will see in Chapter 7, it is not generally supported by Christianity and Islam—let alone our modern scientific community. It also raises the question of what happens to our conscious identity as Individual A, if after our death we are compelled to be born once more as Individual B. How will that conflict be resolved?

We will deal with these questions more deeply in our final chapter, but in the meantime, let us suffice to say that Newton's case studies, first published in 1994, created a sensation. What is particularly fascinating is that these testimonies closely match the near-death experiences reported by NDE patients. As in the case of Sheila and other patients in this chapter, Newton's clients reported that as soon as they died, they found themselves floating over their hospital bed. They saw their loved ones in great distress while doctors frantically tried to resuscitate them. "This is so incredible," one patient said under deep hypnosis, "the nurses are pulling a sheet over my head... I'm supposed to be dead, but I'm still *alive!*"[63] The patient then became aware of his wife, sitting at his bedside, utterly devastated by the loss of her husband. "My wife is sobbing," he said, still in a deep state of hypnosis, "and I am trying to reach into her mind to tell her everything is all right with me... I want her to know my suffering is gone... I'm free of my body ... I don't need it anymore," but his wife is "too overcome with grief."

Newton's patients then went on to describe many of the same feelings experienced by NDE patients. They felt they were drifting, freed from their infirm body, still hovering in the room where they died until some unseen gravity gently tugged them away. In some cases this evolves in a matter of minutes, whereas other patients want to hover around their loved ones for a few hours, or even a few days, up and until the moment of their burial. While for us that seems like a long time, we will see that our measurements of hours or days do not matter in the spiritual universe; there, time is of no consequence.

Eventually, Newton's patients reported drifting through a tunnel towards a great light, exactly as described by NDE patients. Here, they were overwhelmed by feelings of serenity and peace. Prompted by Newton, one patient in deep hypnosis remembered the event as one in which "I feel .. thoughts of love .. companionship ... empathy ... and it's all combined with ... anticipation ... as if others are ... waiting for me."[64] At that point, many described being met by a guide, just as NDE patients reported earlier. Eventually they were introduced to a group of other spirits that they bonded with and that ultimately became their new spiritual family, as we will see in a later chapter.

Michael Newton died in 2016, but his book, *Journey of Souls*, continues to be printed and is now in its fifth edition. This extraordinary success was followed by two other books, *Destiny of Souls* (2001) and *Life between Lives* (2004), each of which provide details of additional case studies whereby patients related their time as spirits in a heavenly universe, in between their lives on earth.

Taken together, this astounding body of near-death and regressive hypnotherapeutic experiences is perhaps our most compelling evidence of the survival of our consciousness after death. But what is this consciousness, exactly? Where does it reside? Is it part of our brain, or separate from our brain?

And can modern neuroscience help us to unlock this riddle?

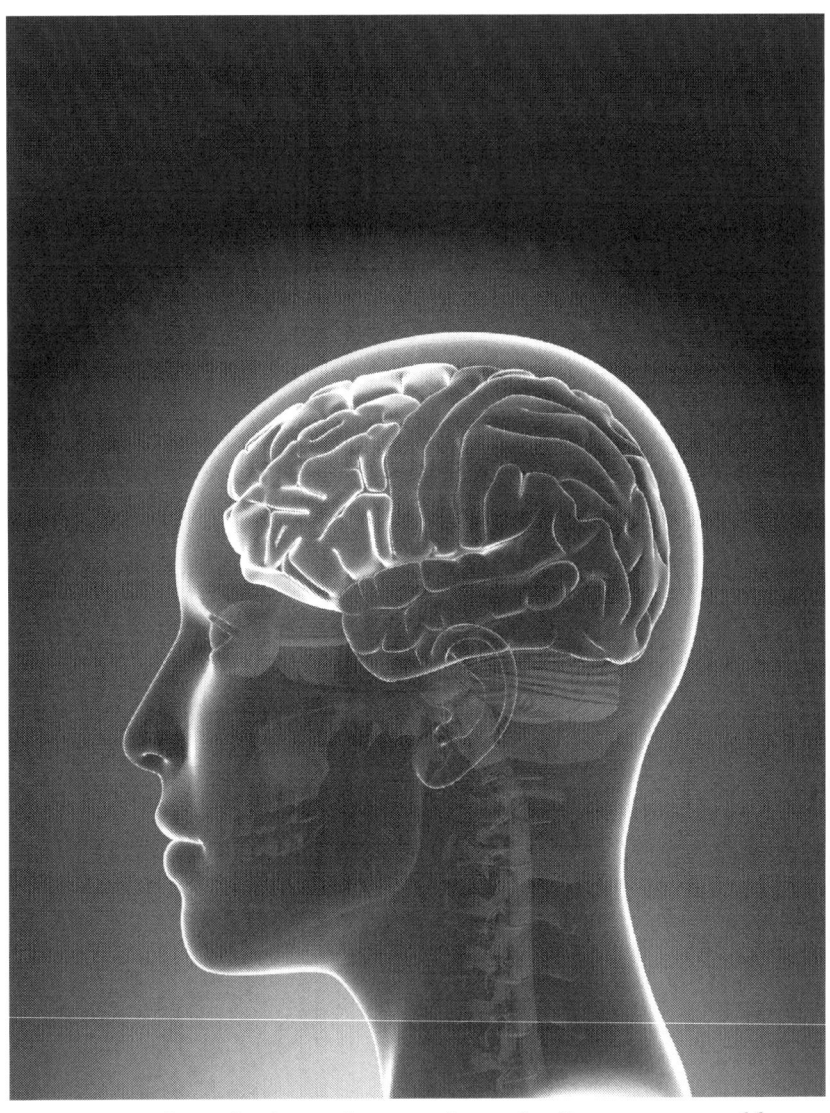

Can modern physics and neuroscience finally answer age-old
questions about the source of human consciousness?

4. The Search for Consciousness

Of all the modern research being conducted about the human brain, perhaps the most elusive question is the role of human consciousness. What is this consciousness, exactly? What makes us a *homo sapiens*, a species blessed with self-awareness? It's a good question. It's also a hard question. So hard, in fact, that scientists have coined a term for it: the Hard Problem of Consciousness, or HPC (no, I'm not kidding; that's what they call it). The reason why it is so hard for scientists to get their head around it is because they insist on approaching the question of consciousness as a problem of matter, to be identified in physical terms. But as we have seen, consciousness is definitely not a physical thing. If it was, it would die when our brain dies. But as we saw in the previous chapter, our consciousness doesn't die. Instead, it continues to function when, by every measure known to man, our brain does not. How can we explain that?

As Charles Tart has noted, something funny happens when physicists and neurologists discuss the human consciousness: they inevitably default to the vernacular of computer science. "Specific conscious processes such as memory, emotions, perception, and so forth merely become subprograms of ordinary consciousness," he writes. Altered states, including dreams and other expressions of the subconsciousness are simply different programs in the operating system that runs on the "hardware" of our human body.

It follows, then, that when this hardware is destroyed, "when the brain and body die, consciousness necessarily dies with them." Or as Tart puts it: mind=brain.[65]

As we have seen, that doesn't explain the vast evidence of near-death and regressive hypnotherapy experiences. Some form of our consciousness must survive to explain the amazing sensations that patients experienced after their body was pronounced dead. But what form does this consciousness take?

To answer this question, the first thing we should recognize is that our consciousness actually consists of a number of things. First, it processes and interprets the vast amount of raw data that our senses perceive, using the computing ability of our brain. Second, it drives the motor functions of our body, including simple things like walking or eating, and more sophisticated functions like speech. As part of that, it also monitors the status of our organs. When any part of our body reports a problem, usually in the form of a pain signal, that part of our consciousness receives the information and prompts a response. Some authors refer to these functions as *qualia*. Interestingly, these are functions that modern robotics and artificial intelligence aim to replicate, and in many cases have succeeded in doing so.

But our consciousness also manages higher level functions. For example, it acts like a "cloud" in which data, such as our memory, our life experience, our knowledge, and our wisdom is stored, collated, and applied in order to filter the constant stream of raw data that our senses take in. Some of that information is stored in our subconscious, while more current data (things we did yesterday, for example) is kept in our immediate "random-access" memory. Our mind uses this accumulated experience to construct and maintain the narrative of our identity: the self-story of who we are, and what motivates us in the decisions we take. That is closely related to another dimension, which is the realm of our emotions: our feelings of love, joy, or sadness, as well as our desire, our hopes and dreams. This set of functions determines our behavior, our character, and our sense of self. Known as our "intentional consciousness," it is a group of functions that are very difficult to replicate in either robotics or artificial intelligence. And finally, there is realm of our unconsciousness or "non-intentional consciousness" which we discussed previously, and which is particularly active during periods of dreamless sleep, or even a coma.[66]

Of course, all of these six levels are closely interrelated. They are not separate computer apps, as some might think, but rather aspects of a deep and dense network of cognitive functioning. But as you probably already recognized, some of these higher functions are directly related to our bodily functions, whereas others are not. Processing the data from our five senses is a very important function while we are alive, but as soon as these senses shut down at our death, that part of our consciousness no longer needs to function. Similarly, at that stage the motor functions that drive our physical movements are no longer required. That doesn't mean that as conscious beings we no longer perceive things in the afterlife, or are unable to move around, since NDE reports show that patients most definitely continue to do that. But they are doing it by other means—in ways that are transcendental rather than physical in nature, as we will see in Chapter 6.

What does conceivably remain, based on these same NDE reports, are higher functions that are not directly linked to our physical functioning. This includes our memory and wisdom; our cognitive ability; and our sense of self. This, then, is the consciousness that I believe is able to survive death and to proceed into a new real, a spiritual realm. As Tart has noted, a close analogy of this particular form of consciousness is our ability to dream. When we dream, we have no immediate awareness of our physical body. Instead, we are guided by images that are spontaneously produced by our unconscious mind. In these dreams, we still retain the sense of self, as well as the ability to process information or move from place to place, but these sensations are entirely divorced from our physical state.[67]

Locating our Consciousness

The question that has vexed physicists and neurologists for many years is, if our consciousness and the human brain are so closely related, where is it? Can we pinpoint our self-awareness anywhere in the physical structure of the brain? Or can we, to put it in scientific terms, identify the neural correlates of consciousness?

To answer that question, we should first understand what neuroscience is and what it tries to do. There is no question that in just the last few decades, neuroscience has advanced by leaps and bounds in our understanding of how the brain works. But we should always remember what we saw in an earlier chapter: that these new disciplines are still very, very young. For example, the discipline of cognitive neuroscience—the interpretation of how we make meaning of what our senses perceive—only emerged in the 1990's after the discovery of a technology called Magnetic Resonance Imaging, or "MRI." Notwithstanding its catchy name, and the fact that it uses a combination of magnetic and electric fields to generate images of the body, an MRI system cannot see sources of energy itself. (Wouldn't it be great if it did! We could have settled this debate a long time ago!)

What MRI scans do look for are protons or hydrogen nuclei in human soft tissue (primarily water and fat), by surrounding a patient with a strong magnetic field. This field makes these protons "spin," or align in such a way that they can be visualized with radio waves, which are both transmitted and received by the MRI scanner. What a radiologist does, in essence, is to manipulate the rate of proton spin in order to generate a contrast between different body tissues. By changing the magnetic field orientation, this technician is thus able to see a particular organ from different angles, and produce an actual three-dimensional view of almost any part of the human body.

Because MRIs works with magnetic fields, the radiologist has to make sure that the patient doesn't have anything that could affect those read-outs, such as jewelry, a mobile phone, keys, or even dental work. A few years ago, I underwent an MRI scan of my brain and forgot to take off my watch. The technician didn't catch it either. Fortunately, the MRI came out fine, but the same could not be said for my watch: it had stopped, and refused to budge. I was very distraught, because the watch was a beautiful Tag Heuer that my wife had given me 25 years ago as an engagement present. But the technician told me not to worry; with a bit of luck, he said, the magnetic alignment of the mechanism would slowly readjust itself to normal earth conditions. And it did: after a few anxious days, the watch started ticking again, and has worked beautifully ever since.

MRI technology was originally developed to see things that

conventional X-rays or CAT scans could not, because these older technologies can only create a limited picture of human soft tissue. X-rays use a small dose of radiation to penetrate the body and "see" the source of a particular injury. CAT Scans essentially work in the same way, by harnessing the power of digital technology to an X-ray. But X-ray radiation can be harmful over the long run. More importantly, these technologies can never create the type of deep contrast that an MRI scanner provides, and that a radiologist needs to develop an accurate diagnosis.

Initially, however, MRI imaging was not very useful for neurologists, because the composition of the human brain is very different than our other organs. Brains are composed of neurons, synapses, and glial cells. In response, scientists developed a new technique called fMRI, or *functional* magnetic resonance imaging. What this process looks for is small changes in blood flow. The theory is that when neurons transmit electrical energy within their circuits, they need to use energy. That energy is delivered by blood flow and quickly metabolized. The trick, of course, is to figure out if that blood flow changes as a result of a particular task, or because of some abnormality. To put that in scientific terms, the question is whether the difference in magnetic susceptibility between oxygenated and deoxygenated hemoglobin can be used as an index of local brain activity. Scientists refer to that differential as the BOLD signal, which stands for "Blood Oxygen Level Dependent." In other words, the BOLD signal is a proxy for measuring neuronal activity related to a particular task or stimulus.

Until the 1990's, the only way to measure brain activity was to use an EEG or Electroencephalography. In that process, tiny electrodes are placed on a patient's scalp to record electrical impulses from the brain. But EEG's suffer from one major drawback, and that is that they cannot locate *where* the neurons are firing in the brain. As a result, it is difficult to correlate these signals to a particular brain function. By contrast, fMRI's can look deep inside a human brain, and create a 3-dimensional image that allow us to hypothesize which neuronal activity is related to which emotional or cognitive response.

Not surprisingly, the development of *f*MRI data acquisition has led to an explosion of interest among neurologists. Until this technology came about, we only had a sketchy idea of how the brain synapses work, and how the brain ages over time. But with *f*MRI scanners, neuroscientists are finally able to measure the biological signals that the human brain produces. That means that scientists can now study cognitive behavior during a variety of different tasks, such as reading a book, or studying a difficult problem, or simply watching television or listening to music. This data can then be used to arrive at some hypotheses about how brain behavior changes, depending on the tasks we ask it to perform.

That, at least, is the theory. In practice, however, the technology is still in its infancy, because we are still learning how to interpret the visual readouts from *f*MRI scans. Very often, artifacts and other imaging issues can confound technicians and lead to incorrect conclusions, simply because our experience with this technology is still so young.[68] Another problem is the limited resolution that today's MRI scans provide. Remember the early days of a PC? Back in the early 1980's, a color image mapped at a resolution of 640 by 480 pixels was a big deal. Similarly, our televisions were square, and were only capable of displaying an image at 720 by 480 pixels. Today, streaming networks routinely broadcast images at four times that size, known as 4K (3840 x 2160 pixels). Our *f*MRI technology must undergo a similar transformation, but that will take time. As a recent paper at the British Royal Society argued, much more detailed *f*MRI scans are needed to accurately capture "the minute magnetic moments of the protons comprising the nuclei of hydrogen atoms in water molecules with feasible applied magnetic fields."[69] Translated into English, that means that we are still far from obtaining the necessary detail to accurately interpret what is going on. For example, today's scans can only see a non-quantitative index in both blood volume and oxygen extraction. A truly quantitative measurement would tell us a lot more about what the brain is doing, and why.

This has not stopped neuro-physicists from embracing *f*MRI scans as the holy grail. In fact, the technology has produced an entirely new field, known as neuroimaging or "brain imaging." The focus of this discipline is on two main outcomes: one, to try to capture a visual image of intracranial diseases, such as brain tumors; and two, to try to discover how the brain resolves certain tasks. It is the latter that is of particular interest to both neurologists and cognitive psychologists, for the truth is that we still don't know how the brain really works. "We don't necessarily know all the brain's hierarchical levels, or how they interact," says psychologist Stuart Hameroff, just as "we don't understand life."[70] We know a lot more than we did just 25 years ago, but we are still learning. And there is much, much more to be discovered.

Part of the problem, says Henry Soper, a neuropsychologist

and author of *Understanding the Frontal Lobe of the Brain*, is that scientists don't even agree on the process of the brain's executive functions. What that means is that there are different theories about the way that the brain processes information, and what role each of the different parts of the brain play in that regard. What we do know is that the so-called frontal lobes of the brain are believed to be responsible for what is known as "higher order functions," such as self-awareness, self-regulation, and intentionality—things that are of great interest to us in this story.[71] But to separate such functions too rigidly from other brain elements carries risk, for if there is one thing we know, it is that all higher functions of the human body tend to work in a complex collaborative system, like the instruments in an orchestra.

Still, these limitations have not stopped some psychologists to develop a science known as neuro-marketing. This is based on the idea that by looking into the brain of a person watching a television commercial, for example, we can "see" how that person responds to the advertising message. As neuropsychologist Christophe Morin has suggested, this could potentially give advertisers an unprecedented edge in predicting the success of their TV commercials and web ads, or even entire movies.[72] At the same time, the idea that advertisers could "peer into" the mind of consumers as they process the daily barrage of commercial information raises some very troubling ethical questions.

Remember the "subliminal message" scare from the 1950's and 1960's? In 1957, a market researcher named James Vicary claimed that he had been able to insert a subliminal message in a film that was then being screened at a movie theater. By briefly flashing frames of Coca Cola and popcorn in the picture, too short for our consciousness to recognize but long enough for our subconsciousness to detect, Vicary hoped to stimulate an intuitive desire among the audience to run to the concession stand and purchase Coke and popcorn in vast quantities.[73]

Never mind that Vicary never provided any evidence for his claims, or that no study has ever been able to replicate the idea of subliminal messaging. The damage was done; particularly in the Zen-like mindset of the '60's and '70s, the idea that evil marketers could prey on the brainwaves of innocent viewers struck a nerve. A study conducted in 1993 showed that many years later, 85% of people still believe that advertisers use subliminal messaging.

Is that true? The answer is: no, for the simple reason that advertisers don't want to "hide" their merchandise. It is far more effective to *show* the product. That is why advertisements in cinemas like to feature close-ups of soda bottles with fresh drops of condensation. It's those images that produce the visceral emotion in our brain that triggers a buying response.

I have told you this short cautionary tale to underscore that today, we really don't know all that much of what goes on in the brain. Part of the reason is its complexity: a typical brain has over 100 billion neurons and trillions of synaptic connections, which together make up the neural circuitry that run our bodies. And although neurons represent only 5% of all cells in the human brain, they actually run the show. That is because they emit small electrical currents that together produce a variety of frequency patterns. These patterns are referred to as "brainwaves" that may reflect a person's emotional and cognitive state.

Neuroscience has certainly lifted a veil on the brain, but what the firing of all these synapses means in qualitative terms is still to be discovered. Psychologist Dr. Robert Lanza phrased it best when he wrote in a recent article that "while neuroscience has made tremendous progress illuminating the functioning of the brain, why we have a subjective experience remains mysterious." Where, he asked, is the "I," the conscious element that "feels and lives life?" Where is our consciousness?

What Lanza is saying is essentially what this book has argued from the beginning: that our consciousness and our brain are *two separate things*. While the brain certainly facilitates our thinking as a homo sapiens, it is only the vessel, the executive branch that "operates" our body. Our consciousness is a separate entity, for as the evidence in this book has shown, it operates on a much more dynamic level. Of course, that's not what our scientific community believes. Most physicists staunchly argue that our brain and our consciousness are one and the same. Therefore, when our brain dies, so do we.

This, then, is the ultimate enigma that has bedeviled humankind: Are the mind and the brain one and the same, or not? It is a question that philosophers and physicians have debated for centuries, ever since the French 17th century philosopher René Descartes formulated the Cartesian dualism, arguing that the two are fundamentally different: an immaterial mind, working closely with a material brain.[74] But modern secular physics reject that notion.

What has happened, however, is that *f*MRI technology has moved this debate firmly into the neurological domain, spawning academic journals such as the *Neuroscience of Consciousness*, published by Oxford University. Much of the current academic debate in these journals revolves around ideas such as the

Integrated Information Theory, or IIT. IIT, a cornerstone of reductionist thinking about human awareness, posits that consciousness is an intrinsic and fundamental property of its physical, organic system.[75] It does so on the basis of five "axiomatic assumptions," meaning that all higher levels of consciousness, including *intrinsic existence, composition, information, integration* and *exclusion* require physical mechanisms to survive and operate. But this theory is purely hypothetical; no brain scan has ever proven that this is indeed the case.

Other scientists have tried to chart a compromise between reductionism and dualism. They believe that if our head contains both the organic brain and the non-organic spiritual mind, there's got to be a way of locating the darn thing. Some have even suggested that the pineal gland may be the bridge between the physical and spiritual dimension of our consciousness. Why the pineal gland? The simple answer is that scientists don't know what it is supposed to do. But they do know that it is located at the very center of our brain, and that unlike all other brain organs, it is not paired in a left/right configuration. It is, quite literally, the "cockpit" of the human brain. Clinical psychiatrist Rick Strassman believes he has discovered the reason why there could be a spiritual dimension to this organ: it produces a chemical called Di-Methyl Tryptamine or DMT, which can induce a person into a psychedelic or transcendental experience.[76] But scholars have known about such ideas for a long time. As early as the 17th century, Descartes theorized that the pineal gland was the "seat of the soul."

Another theory, developed in the 1990's by Dr. Hameroff and Sir Roger Penrose, a mathematical physicist at Oxford University, is that our consciousness is actually stored in micro-tubules, as part of a "program" run by a quantum computer inside the brain (here we go again). Micro-tubules are microscopic tubular structures that can be found in the cytoplasm of cells, and the idea that they can store information *inside* the neuron, rather than as a function of connections *between* neurons, is known as "orchestrated objective reduction" or Orch-OR. That in itself is not a terribly groundbreaking idea, except for the fact that the authors believe that when the brain dies, these microtubules retain the information stored within.[77] As Hameroff explained on a recent Science Channel documentary, "Let's say that the heart stops beating, the blood stops flowing; the micro-tubules lose their quantum state. The quantum information within the micro-tubules is not destroyed, it can't be destroyed, and it just distributes and dissipates to the universe at large."[78] That is an interesting concept, but it doesn't explain how, exactly, the information from the micro-tubules is "dissipated" to the universe.

The bottom line, as Descartes wrote, is that "I think, therefore I know I exist" (*je pense, donc je suis*). Everything else is up for grabs. We know we are conscious beings, that we can see, touch, smell, and hear things, but exactly how this information is processed in a way that makes us aware of ourselves is still a mystery. Neuroscience has lifted a veil on our brain, in the sense that we can see more than we ever could in the past; but correlating brainwaves with particular functions of human consciousness still eludes us. Or as J. Allan Hobson writes in *Towards a Science of Consciousness*, "Philosophical and experimental psychological approaches have failed in their efforts to clearly define, let alone explain, human consciousness."[79]

This has prompted neurologist Jay Lombard, author of *The Mind of God*, to go as far as to claim that "Neuroscientists don't believe that such a thing as the mind exists. They flat-out reject the concept of the mind. I find that a very scary, slippery slope."[80]

That may be true, but to some extent I cannot blame neuroscientists for not daring to go beyond the limitations of their reductionist beliefs. They are not philosophers; their principal task is to discover ways to alleviate serious conditions such as head injury, brain impairment, and illnesses such as Alzheimer's Disease. The greater question of what drives our consciousness and our universe is not very often on the agenda of university labs that depend on research grants to stay in business.

But you and I have no such constraints. We don't have to worry about securing the next pharmaceutical research grant, or whether our academic tenure is in danger (well, I do of course, but that's a different story). That means that we don't have the limitations that is holding back a majority of modern scientists—including neuroscientists—who must operate within the ramifications of what today is considered acceptable scholarship. Instead, we can open our mind and our heart without the fear of anyone calling us out or ridiculing us at an academic symposium. Or to take it one step further, we can openly consider the possibility that we don't understand human consciousness *precisely because it is not of a human origin*.

The View of Quantum Physics

This is not as outlandish as you may think. In fact, support for this idea can once again be found in quantum physics. As Audrey Ordenes has noted, what do classical physics do best? They do really well when trying to explain fixed macroscopic phenomena, such as measuring the trajectory of a rocket. Remember those formulas that we had to calculate in physics' class, to determine acceleration, the mass of an object, or the net force acting upon an object? Well, these formulas work perfectly when measuring phenomena that can be observed. But they utterly fall apart when the object in question gets close to the speed of light, when matter becomes a function of energy. The reason is that according to quantum physics, the position and momentum of the particle can't both be known at the same time.

To explain this, remember that everything in quantum physics has a wave function—such as an electron—that determines its behavior. This is known as the wave-particle duality: the idea that all matter and all energy sometimes behave like waves, and sometimes like particles. Of course, that fuzzy concept is not very satisfactory, which is why the Austrian scientist Erwin Schrödinger developed the so-called Schrödinger Equation. His theory postulates that if you determine the wave function of a particle, you will also have the probability of finding that particle at a certain position. In sum, it helps to define the probability density of a particle in space and time.

If this sounds like gobbledygook to you, don't worry; you're not the only one. Few people agree what quantum physics are actually about, including quantum physicists themselves. For example, Werner Heisenberg argued that you *can't* have it both ways. If you try to measure the position of an electron, for example, you will not be able to identify its momentum as well. In other words, the safe, comfortable world of conventional laboratory physics, where everything can be neatly pinned down and measured, no longer applies to the strange new world of quantum physics.

As a result, quantum physicists are far more likely to peek over the fence of their discipline, so to speak, and mess around with things like philosophy or metaphysics, which are the bane of any traditional scientist. As physicist Bernard d'Espagnat wrote, perhaps quantum theory can close the gap between reductionist science and the "God's eye view" of reality.[81] One example is the famous Copenhagen interpretation, which essentially says that trying to measure nature is ultimately doomed to failure. Just the act of trying to measure a system, says Copenhagen, is bound to lead to a wave function collapse. Copenhagen's lead scientist was Niels Bohr, whom we quoted previously. Translated into plain English, what Bohr is saying is that while we can try to observe things, we should never assume that this observation will reveal the full totality of their complexity.

According to Kimberly Cantergiani, one example of this weird complexity is a particular interpretation of quantum physics, much beloved by science-fiction writers, known as the "many-worlds interpretation." As described in Adam Becker's book *What is Real?* this particular theory suggests that every quantum event is essentially a fork in the road with multiple possible outcomes.[82] According to this interpretation, every fork could potentially produce a new universe, and every quantum event could in theory be replicated on every star, in every galaxy.

True, this idea may be too bizarre to take seriously. But there is no question that of all scientists, quantum scholars are the only ones prepared to examine ideas that do not conform to the rule book of traditional physics. Rather than looking for hard measurements, they try to look for things that no physics class has ever taught us: they search for *meaning*.

Where to find such meaning? Where can we find evidence for the idea that the mind is *not* made of matter? The answer, I think, is to visit a world that has rarely been featured in scholarly discussions about human consciousness, or the possibility of its post-mortem existence: the world of the psychic experience.

Adam's finger touches the hand of God in Michelangelo's
Creation of Adam, 1512.

5. The Psychic Experience

Even as a very young child, Sue knew things and saw things that her siblings didn't. When she was a toddler of barely two, she would stand in her crib and cry for her favorite doll because her mother couldn't find it. But the point was, little Sue *did*. From her vantage point, high up in the ceiling in the adjoining room, she could see exactly where her doll was. The problem was, she couldn't explain that to her Mom, for she didn't know the words.

What Sue was experiencing, of course, was an Out of Body Experience (OBE), similar to the ones we saw in a previous chapter, as part of Near Death Experiences. But OBEs —or what the medical community refers to as autoscopy or veridical experiences—are not limited to the dying process. The ability of a living person to seemingly leave one's body and see things from a different perspective has been widely reported in the scientific literature. In a 1984 study, author Susan Blackmore estimated that one in every ten persons will have such an experience at least once in a lifetime.[83] In most cases, however, such veridical experiences are induced by a variety of unusual circumstances, such as brain trauma, severe concussion, sensory deprivation, the use of psychedelic drugs or hallucinogens, or simply a lack of sleep.[84]

I vividly remember my own OBE, which took place in France in 2001. I had flown without sleep for nearly two days to attend the famous television festival, known as MIPCOM, in the French coastal resort of Cannes. Along the way, I discovered that people were extremely tense. It was just a few weeks after the 9/11 attacks, and all airports were on a high state of alert. My plane from Los Angeles, which should have been packed with all sorts of Hollywood types, was nearly empty. But when I finally arrived in my hotel in the nearby town of Juan-les-Pins, I couldn't sleep. The tension that had built up during the long flight refused to give my brain a rest. And so I spent the night tossing and turning while trying everything I knew to fall asleep: push-ups, reading, praying, or meditating. Nothing worked.

Then, around 5:00am, as dawn was slowly breaking over the Mediterranean, I saw two spirits come into my room. They took me by the arm and carried me aloft as if it was the most normal thing in the world. I was astonished, and of course I didn't have a clue as to what was happening. But at the same time, it seemed quite normal to be flying with these two beings—angels?—on either side of me. Neither of them spoke; they just smiled and took me on the most incredible journey I have ever experienced. We soared over the snowcapped summit of the Alpes-Maritimes, swooped down to the fields and rocky escarpments of the Provence, and skimmed low over the blue waters of the Mediterranean—so close that I felt the spray of the waves on my face. It was an incredible ride, and to this day I still remember the sensation of the wind ruffling my hair (yes, I still had hair at that time).

Then, as suddenly as they had appeared, the spirits brought me back to my body in my little hotel room, and I woke up. I looked at the clock, and realized that I could not have been asleep for more than 30 minutes. But amazingly, I felt as refreshed and energized as if I had a full, 8-hour night's sleep. I was so astonished and giddy that I immediately called my wife Cathie, who was surprised to get a call from Europe so late in the day. I breathlessly told her about my experience, but I wasn't sure if she believed me (today, she swears that she did). But the most incredible thing is that I spent all of that day on the floor of the Palais de Congrès, taking meetings, without any sense of jet lag or fatigue. Usually, I'm a wreck after flying from Los Angeles to Europe. But that day, I felt as new and refreshed as if I'd just had a long vacation.

As my story, and that of countless other veridical experiences illustrate, for the vast majority of us an OBE is a singular event. It is not something that we experience on a daily basis, as a matter of course; only an exceptional circumstance can bring it on. For Sue, however, it is quite different. As far back as she can remember, she had veridical experiences that felt very natural to her. She thought—as only young children can—that being able to travel out of your body and see things from a different viewpoint was something that all human beings are able to do.

One day, it got her into trouble. Her parents were planning to host a fancy dinner party. All day long, the house was in a state of frenzy as meals were cooked and the dining room was cleaned and dressed. Shortly before the guests were due to arrive, all the children were bathed and packed off to bed. Everyone, including little Sue, was warned they were not allowed to get out of bed under any circumstance, unless it involved a dire emergency.

And then, the doorbell rang, the first guests arrived, and the evening began. Wine flowed, the food was wonderful, and everyone had a good time—including, as it happened, Sue's little dog. With all those wonderful smells wafting about, the dog felt that it should be entitled to have a bite as well, and so it did. When it thought no one was looking, the pup snatched a succulent piece of steak from the dish of one of the guests, who was deeply absorbed in conversation with her neighbor. No one noticed the dog's surreptitious move, except Sue's mother. Sue's Mom saw everything. And so did little Sue, as it turned out, from high above, during one of her usual Out-of-Body Experiences.

The next morning, she ran down to tell her Mom. "Did you see what the dog did?" she said. "She's so naughty, stealing that piece of meat!"

Her mother was very cross with her. "I thought I told you to stay in bed!" she said. "Did you sneak down and look through the glass door?"

"But I didn't!" Sue cried with a trembling lip. "I just saw what happened."

It was only much later that Sue realized that children do *not* have the ability that she had; that kids only see what is in front of their eyes, and that no one can simply wander out of their body to find out what is happening next door. It shocked her, for children don't normally question what they see.

"I always felt that there was a sense of *belonging* around me, a sense of an energy that was much bigger than me or the people around me," she remembers. "And as a child, this was something that I took for granted. I often felt like coming out of my body, for my mother would put me to bed long before I felt any inclination to sleep. I actually thought I could fly, because I would go out and tour the area around our neighborhood in Manchester, where we lived. I have so many memories of those experiences, even today, but now I realize how remarkable they are, because they're all from what you'd call a "bird's eye view," looking down. There is no way a young child could have had those experiences. And yet, I did."

As Sue grew into a teen, she realized something else: she was starting to have premonitions. "It is very difficult to describe," she told me. "It's like a feeling that wells up inside of you, spontaneously. It's like a thought process, except it originates from the outside. It just comes. From one moment to the next, it's on your mind."

For example, she described how, at age six, she was in a car accident. Nobody was using seat belts then, not even young children. So one day, she was in her mother's car when it hit another vehicle and she slammed her head against the dashboard.

Naturally, her mother was frantic. An ambulance was called. Sue was placed on a gurney, and everyone was in a panic. Except Sue herself. "I had no fear," she says, "because I knew, simply *knew*, that everything would be all right, that my injury wasn't serious, and that there was no reason to be upset. And so I remember being quite relaxed and smiling while I watched all these adults running around and fussing over me. I also noticed that one of the two men who carried my stretcher into the ambulance had a very funny-looking beard. He looked like a cartoon figure with that weird beard and his hair sticking out. And I couldn't help myself—I started to laugh. Of course, that made everyone even more upset—they thought I was delirious or something."

When Sue was 13, there came a turning point. It began to dawn upon her that she might be spiritually gifted; that she felt and saw things, *spiritual* things. She was intelligent enough to recognize those talents for what they are: that she was psychic. Her mother had noticed this as well, as mothers invariably do, and was in awe of that idea—that her daughter could be so extraordinarily gifted. But as so often happens in the development of an adolescent girl, Sue didn't think this was a particularly desirable thing to have. She wanted to be like the other girls in her class. Some of the premonitions she felt—particularly about what was happening in other places in the world, in regions torn apart by war or famine— were so uncomfortable that it depressed her. One day she experienced the suffering of an African village with such intensity that she took all of the money she had saved up, and sent it to an African relief organization. That was the final straw.

"I tried to shut down everything," she remembers. "I realized I didn't want to be a psychic or a special healer. I didn't want to be involved in all of that. I just wanted to be *normal*."

For the next few years she rigorously tried to suppress all of these feelings and premonitions, and live like a normal person. She graduated from high school and went to college, earning a degree in mathematics. Soon thereafter, she found herself in a classroom, teaching children the fundamentals of arithmetic. And, she says, that's when her psychic abilities came back full force.

"Here I was," she says, "trying to teach these kids the basics of math with these stupid text books that were written as if they were adults! And I keenly felt, as clear as the light of day, that that's *not* at all how I should teach those kids. I felt an incredible urge to climb on top of my desk and start to sing, or jump down to the front of the class and do a little dance, or take them outside and let them count the leaves of a flower. *That's* how kids discover things. That's how they learn. I felt it so keenly, how these young minds ached to know things, but in a playful way. And so I threw all the math books out the window, and I started to tell them *stories*. I never worried about how I should organize my thoughts or design a particular curricular approach, because I knew that as soon as I opened my mouth, the stories would well up inside of me. It was almost as if someone else was cuing me. And all the parents were amazed, for guess what: everyone in that class passed their math tests. And the reason is, that for these children the process had become effortless. They never realized that they were *learning*. They were simply enjoying the stories."

Now that she was an accomplished young woman, Sue decided to no longer fight her psychic abilities, but to embrace them. And so, when she felt a growing sense that she should continue her education, she didn't hesitate. She went to Oxford and got a Master's degree in forensic osteo-archaeology: the study of animal and human bones. But her choice for this rather esoteric discipline would have far-reaching consequences.

One night, while living in a quaint 16th century cottage, she had an amazing transformative experience. "I know this sounds strange," she says; "it is difficult to describe, and even more difficult to comprehend. I sat in my chair, reading a book, and all of a sudden, I saw these pink and purple shapes. It looked as if it was raining sheets of yellow, pink and violet in my room. And I thought, "Oh my God, am I losing my mind? Am I having a stroke of some sort?"

"But actually, the vision was very calm and soothing; there was nothing disturbing about it. And then I received the thought that what I was seeing were forms of energy. The same energy, that same spiritual force that had been with me all my life, even when I was a young child. Except now, for the first time, I was not only able to feel it, but *see* it. It simply took my breath away. And at that moment I understood that this was the source of all the premonitions and guidance that I had received over the years. And I knew why this energy had decided to reveal itself for me. Because this was my destiny."

It was a watershed moment, and it would change her life forever.

The Guidance of Spirits

Ancient and medieval literature is full of stories of people who receive guidance from a spirit. That is the real meaning of word "inspiration," based on the Latin verb *inspirare,* which literally means "breathing into" someone—as if someone whispered in your ear. The Greeks thought that such whispers came from their gods, such as Apollo, the god of oracles, or Athena, the goddess of wisdom. In Hebrew Scripture, the prophets call it the voice of God. Christians believe such moments come from the Holy Spirit.

In my book *Ten Prayers that Changed the World,* I tell several stories of people who received such divine whispers and went on to do extraordinary things. One of these was a 13-year old peasant girl named *Jeanne d'Arc*, or Joan of Arc. One day, she heard the spirit tell her "that the day will come when you have to come to France." Joan lived during the period of the pitiless Hundred Years' War, when the English King Henry V joined with Burgundy to attack the French crown prince, the *Dauphin*. As it happened, Joan's parental home was perched on the fault line of that war: the Meuse River, which separated the Burgundians from the Armagnacs, who remain loyal to the French Crown.

The spirits became ever more insistent. "You have to go to Orléans," they urged Joan later that summer. "Go to Orléans to raise the siege that the English have laid around the city." An utterly absurd idea, of course. How was a 13-year old, and a *girl* on top of that, with no education, no military training, and no backing whatsoever, going to lead an army to Orléans? How exactly was that supposed to happen?

But the amazing thing is, she did. The spirits gave Joan the courage to go and plead her case to a captain of the French forces, Robert de Baudricourt, who was stationed in a nearby town. Of course, after listening to her for five minutes, Robert threw her out on the street. But Joan was persistent. She continued to harass him until, one day, the spirits told her an unusual prophecy. She was to go back and warn Robert that an ambush that the French were planning would go badly. Robert was surprised and intrigued. How did this little twerp know that they were planning an attack on an English supply train? But he was even more astonished when later that day, a messenger arrived with the news that the English had put up a stout defense, and that the French raiding party was defeated. It gave him pause. In the end, he did take Joan to the court of the Dauphin.

Here, another test awaited her. The French prince had hidden himself among a crowd of finely dressed noblemen and courtiers. Not knowing what he looked like, Joan was taken aback. But the spirits led her to identify him without fail. Soon, all of the French court was abuzz with talk about *la Pucelle*, the little maid who was clearly divinely inspired. And in the end, Joan got her army. On April 29, 1429, she arrived in Orléans at the head of a convoy that carried desperately needed supplies for the besieged city.

Cheering wildly, the population received her as a savior. But the English were not yet ready to give up. A major battle ensued. After several days of hard fighting, when it seemed that the English were winning, Joan rallied her forces with her battle cry *Ou Nom Dei*, "In the name of God." The English were defeated, and the siege of Orléans was lifted.

Another individual who seemed to be guided by spirits was Martin Luther. In 1521, he was ordered to appear before a tribunal headed by Emperor Charles V, to defend his "heretical" views on the papacy and the church. All of Europe held its breath. If this rebellious Augustinian monk decided to recant, Catholicism in Europe might yet be saved. But if he stood fast, he would likely be burned as a heretic, and a great schism would tear the continent apart.

The first day of the trial, held in the town of Worms on the Rhine, was not auspicious. Luther was not a very impressive figure to look at, with his brown habit, an unruly mop of dark hair, and small, deep-set eyes, hooded by bushy eyebrows. The lords looked at each other and said, "Is this the man who wants to destroy the Church?" They shook their heads and laughed. From there it went from bad to worse. When the prosecutor, bishop Johann von Eck, began to interrogate him, Luther could do little more than mumble, admitting that the books that espouse his views were indeed written by his own hand.

That night, Martin realized that his life, and his life's purpose, hung by a thread. He stayed up most of the night, surrendering himself to prayer. He begged the spirit to pour its wisdom into his heart, and give him the power of speech. Christianity has strayed too far from its mission, he prayed, with Medici popes in Rome that use their office to extort the faithful, to build lavish palaces, and to raise huge armies. That was definitely *not* what Jesus intended. The church, he knew, must return to the Gospels, and stand for love, faith, and justice. That was the thrust of the Ninety-Five Theses that he'd nailed to the door of the castle church of Wittenberg.

True enough, the figure who presented himself to the imperial tribunal the next day was a changed man. Clear of purpose, he stood tall with a light in his eyes. "Yes, these books are all mine," he declared in a strong voice. And with that, he launched into his defense with such passion that the German princes on the panel found themselves swayed by his views. At the end of his oration, Luther declared, "My conscience is captive to the word of God. I cannot and I will not recant anything. Here I stand. I cannot do otherwise."

With these words, Europe would change beyond recognition. Most German princes broke away from Rome and established a Lutheran Church in their domains. At the same time, the schism gave reform-minded Catholic prelates the courage to confront the abuses of the Renaissance popes. A long period of Catholic restoration began, culminating in the Council of Trent.

Reading these stories, you might get the impression that divine whispers are a thing of the past. But the opposite is true. In 1946, for example, a 36-year-old woman found herself on a train traveling through a patchwork of cotton fields of West Bengal in India. She was seated in third class, but up close it was hard to tell. The war had ravaged the rolling stock of the Indian railroad, so that the train was an odd assortment of dilapidated cars and threadbare furnishings—not unlike the state of the British Empire itself at that time.

Seated on a hardwood bench, the young woman was surrounded by humanity in all its forms: farmers with their hens, mothers with their babies, soldiers with rifles, on leave from the fighting in Kashmir. They looked askance at this young woman dressed in the habit of a nun. With her dark East European complexion, one could easily take her for a Bengali native. But in fact, the woman was Albanian, a native of Skopje, from a land now known as Yugoslavia. She was also very ill, which is why her convent in Calcutta had urged her to take a vacation in the cool fields and pastures of Darjeeling.

It was there, in that dirty carriage, that she heard the whispers of a spirit. The voice was direct, explicit, and full of authority. "I was sure it was God's voice," she would later say. "It was a command. I was to leave everything in order to help the poor, and live among them." And so she did. She left her order (a hugely difficult process in itself) and set herself up in a ramshackle building in the Motijhil district of Calcutta. There, she spent her days dispensing food and medication to the countless poor and destitute who lived in the raw sewage of the streets. Before long, the world would learn of her astonishing exploits, and call her Mother Teresa, the modern saint.

Was this courageous Albanian woman an exception? Does it require special gifts to hear and understand the whispers from the spirit? Sue believes the answer is, *no*. As a scientist, she is convinced that each of us has the capacity to hear what our spirit guide is trying to convey. The famous American psychic Edgar Cayce taught that, while not everyone is born with natural psychic ability, everyone has the power to develop that greater spiritual awareness. That is why in cultures around the world, including Asia, Africa, Australasia as well as among Native American tribes, those with a particular ability to hear and interpret these whispers are treated with great respect. They are usually revered as *shamans*, people with the ability to communicate with the spirit world. The root of the word *shaman* is "one who knows." That may explain why there are so few shamans in modern Western culture, because we no longer believe in spirits. We are much more comfortable with material things—things we can touch, smell, eat or wear. That is why the eminent psychologist Gardner Murphy, when asked what the next step in afterlife research should be, replied: "the discovery of powerful mediums."[85]

Sue is such a medium—or to use a better term, a *psychic*—and that is why I realized that I could never write this book without her help. As Sue told me, she only became fully aware of her destiny during that night in her tiny home, as she watched the colorful cloud unfold. She knew then that there was no turning back. She had an exceptional gift, and whether she liked it or not, she was predestined to use that gift and help those in need.

"What really brought it home for me," she says, "what really became the catalyst, was what happened after I saw the colorful rain in my room. I was working on my Master's thesis, and I was trying to identify some bones that had been dug up in Somerset, that my tutor had given me. The problem was, as soon as I brought these bones home, all sorts of bizarre things started to happen. My Internet stopped working. My car wouldn't start. I had mechanics and tech people come over, and they couldn't find anything wrong. Then I found out something that really scared me: two specialists who had previously worked on these bones had had a heart attack. Both of them. They never finished their analysis. Which is why these bones had never been studied properly. It reminded me of that story from the 1920's: the discovery of the tomb of Tutankhamun and the 'curse of the pharaoh'." As you know, Lord Carnarvon, who financed the expedition, died shortly after the burial chamber was opened."

Could the same be true with these bones? Were they cursed in some way?

"In the end," Sue continues, "I asked the spirits to help me. I meditated deeply and waited for the spirits to bring me the knowledge I needed to solve this mystery. And they did. Suddenly I saw what had happened to these bones. They were the bones of young children. And I immediately recognized the signs of severe trauma. I saw how some of these children had been beheaded, while others had been struck with a sword. And I realized that these were the victims of a terrible massacre that had followed the Roman invasion of Britain in 43 A.D. I was seeing the battle before my eyes, and I saw how these poor children were being murdered by Roman troops. And I understood what had happened: the intense horror of those events still lingered in the energy field of the bones. So I prayed over them and bade the spirits to give them rest. And after that, all of the problems in my house went away. The car started again, the Internet came up, and all was fine. And when I finished my Master's thesis, it received the highest grade ever given to a Master's work at my university."

Of course, Sue never revealed the source of her research, for fear that she would be ridiculed. "Never in a million years would I dream of telling my professors of how I got this information," she says. "But sometimes I would slip up. I was working as a researcher and lecturer at Winchester University when one day they brought in this box of animal bones. And right away I saw what type of bones these were, and where they were from, without opening the box. And I cried out, "Oh my God, these are the bones of that fox they dug up at the ancient hillfort." And the man who delivered the box was stunned. He looked at me and said, "hey mate, how the hell do you know that? You haven't even opened the box."

From that moment on, Sue realized, she no longer needed to summon the spirits when she needed them. The vision, the knowledge, would emerge spontaneously.

"I have a dear friend of mine named Pam, who has a dog," she says. "She loves that dog to distraction. She drives all over town with her dog in the back, and the two are a very familiar sight in the place where I live. They are inseparable. But one day, a friend of hers asked if she could borrow Pam's car for the afternoon, and of course Pam agreed. So the friend came and picked up the car, did whatever she had to do, and then returned the car later that day. But then something really weird happened. Late that evening, as Pam got ready to take her dog to the park, he refused to get into the car. He would stand near the open hatchback, but refused to jump in. Pam couldn't believe it. She tried to entice him with treats, which usually worked like a charm, but even that failed to move her dog. He just stood there, trembling slightly, rooted to the ground, refusing to go in.

This went on for several days, and at last Pam turned to me. "Can you help me?" she asked. "I've been driving with that dog for years, but all of a sudden, he won't go in the car. Even if I try to lift him up, he will fight me for all it's worth. I'm at my wit's end. What on earth is wrong with him?"

So I agreed to come over, and as soon as I approached the car, I felt a deep and disturbing sensation. The back of the car, where her dog usually sat, was filled with distressed energy—a force so strong that it was almost physically repulsive.

"What's wrong?" Pam asked, seeing my reaction.

"Did you do anything strange with this car?" I asked. "Did you carry a dead animal or something? Like a bird or a cat that had been run over?"

"Of course not," Pam retorted. "I would know if I did." But then she stopped, tilted her head, and said, "Huh."

"What?" I asked. "Do you remember something?"

"No," she said, "but I gave my car to Amy, a friend of mine. She asked if she could borrow it for the afternoon."

"And what did she do with it?" I asked.

"I don't know, but I will find out," she said, and ran back to her house, looking for her phone.

Eventually her friend Amy was tracked down. And as soon as she found out what we wanted to know, she was deeply apologetic. "I'm so sorry," she said. "I should have told you, but I didn't want to upset you."

"Upset me, how?"

"Well," Amy replied, "our dog wasn't doing so well, and so we decided to take her to the vet to be euthanized. That's why I asked if I could borrow your car, because mine was in the shop. But we didn't want to wait any longer."

Then it all became clear to me. Amazingly, the distress of Amy's dog in the car, on its way to the vet to be put to sleep, had left an imprint of deeply negative energy. That explained why my friend's dog did not want to get in. As soon as it got near, it had sensed that negative energy, left by the fear of that other animal. Incredible, isn't it?"

So Sue went to the back of the car, made contact with the energy, and cleared it. She then asked Pam to go and fetch her dog. Moments later, the dog came running outside, his tongue hanging out, and jumped into the back of the car without another thought. Case solved.

"What that story shows us," she continues, "is that animals are much better at using their senses than we are. I think we are very naïve when we think that animals just perceive what is in front of their eyes. They have a much broader sense of perception, to the point that it can sense energy fields that most of us wouldn't even know about."

To which I might add: you can fool a person, but you can never fool a dog.

The Mystery of Electro-Magnetic Vibrations

What are we to make of these stories? They confirm that not only humans but also animals are made of matter and spirit, and that very often, animals can sense forms of energy that are well beyond our human ability to perceive. Some scientists have woken up to this as well. The result is a new discipline called neuroethology. Founded by a group of European neuropsychologists (including Karl von Frisch and Jörg-Peter Ewert), neuroethology looks at the way that the nervous system of animals responds to all sorts of stimuli in its environment.[86] One example is the way bats have a unique auditory system that allows them to map their navigation based on the acoustic return of sounds.

Here is another striking example. According to a report by

National Geographic, a large swarm of animals fled to the interior before a giant tsunami rolled towards the coasts of Sri Lanka and India in 2005. Inside Sri Lanka's Yala National Park near Patanangala beach, elephants screamed and ran inland; flamingos left their breeding grounds; zoo animals ran into their shelters and refused to come out. But this is the clincher: witnesses say that the animal stampede began *a full hour* before the tsunami hit. No one knew what was about to happen, but the animals did.

Tragically, around 60 park visitors were washed away by the killer waves, but surprisingly few animal carcasses were found, even though the region is a sanctuary to over 130 different species of birds, as well as leopards, goats and water buffalo.[87] The conclusion is inevitable: the incoming danger must have changed the electromagnetic vibrations of the energy field near Patanangala beach. These vibrations were promptly understood by the animals, but not by any humans. Even as the locals went on with their day as if nothing was wrong, animals both large and small fled inland—and were thus largely spared from the disaster.

Most human beings are not sufficiently sensitive to these signals. But some psychics, such as Sue, most definitely are. They are able to sense electromagnetic changes in our energy fields, and decode the information that it contains—as intuitive thoughts or whispers, in much the same way that the animals of Sri Lanka were guided by intuition. That gives psychics a unique window on the spiritual dimension of daily life—not only their own lives, but also the lives of people they come into contact with.

I experienced that unusual sensation first hand. One day, my wife Cathie came home with the news that while she was visiting with her friend Enisa, she had met this remarkable woman named

Sue Jones. Once they got to talk, Sue immediately sensed Cathie's energy. To everyone's surprise, she proceeded to tell Cathie things that no one—other than me and she—could ever know. For example, she told her that our marriage was blessed with love and happiness, but that there were things on my mind that worried me—even though Sue had never met me in my life. And then she proceeded to give Cathie chapter and verse about all the things that weighed on me, and often prevented me from getting a good night sleep. I was astonished. Apart from Cathie and my doctor, no one knew about my struggles with insomnia.

Of course, as soon as I heard the story, I insisted that I meet Sue myself. And thanks to our friend Enisa, a meeting was arranged the very next day. That's how our collaboration started.

You would think that this phenomenon—that some people can see our most intimate energy fields—would be a source of tremendous interest to the scientific community. But as we saw in previous chapters, that is rarely the case. In our modern society, the suggestion that someone may have psychic abilities is usually met with skepticism, in sharp contrast to the status that psychics enjoyed in other cultures. The reason is not only our deeply vested attachment to physical reality, and the distrust of anything that challenges that belief; it is also the result of the way our media, including television, have exploited magicians, mediums and fortune-tellers purely for their entertainment value. Our culture has trivialized the talent of psychics, because deep in our hearts we are uncomfortable with the idea that some people can sense things that we can't.

What has further discouraged scientific research in this area is that there are no predictors for whether a person has paranormal aptitude or not. Psychologists have a very hard time coming to grips with that. In psychology, scholars use *quantitative* surveys to look for patterns that can be decoded and generalized for the population at large, and ultimately used in therapeutic practice. I know, for I spent ten years of my academic career supervising dissertations in psychology. But the problem is, psychics don't conform to patterns as a function of the general population. Genuine psychics are rare, and seem to appear at random. A case in point is a 2011 study by Cornell University's Daryl Bem, who found that out of 1,000 participants, only 8 showed "significant statistical evidence for precognition and premonition." Though that number was small, Bem was surprised that this many people were shown to have any paranormal ability at all.[88]

Another problem with scientific research in psychic ability is that these are typically focused on artificial "tests;" for example, to determine whether psychics can "see" an object that is hidden from them. Again, this is a reflection of our culture's obsession with magic tricks. In one such study, conducted in 2012 by the University of London, two psychics were asked to identify people seated behind a curtain. They couldn't. The reason, which apparently the researchers never understood, is that bona fide psychics don't *control* what they see, because they are not the ones doing the actual "seeing"; they only perceive what their energy or "spirit" is allowing them to see. Here, again, the unpredictability of the psychic experience, precisely because it is dependent on spiritual intervention, confounds scholars who want things to be nice and tidy.

Recognizing this problem, a group of other studies have begun to look at the question whether people actually *believe* in paranormal phenomena. Perhaps they thought that if a sufficiently large number of people accept the possibility of psychic ability, it must be true. Exactly such a study was conducted in 2006, using a sample of 439 college students in Oklahoma (why college students, you ask? Why not a sample from the general population? The answer: because it is more convenient for professors). The study found that belief in psychic ability seemed to increase as students advanced in their academics: while only 23% of undergraduate students expressed such a belief, among graduate students that faith had increased to 34%. It also revealed that social science students are more likely to have trust in paranormal talent than science students, which may not be surprising.[89]

The same question was asked in a 2005 Gallup poll among a general sample of the United States population, and this time the number of those who believed in extrasensory perception was considerably higher: some 41%.[90] A CBS News survey conducted four years later found that the number had increased to 57%. Interestingly, this survey also confirmed the Oklahoma finding that belief in psychic phenomena seems to increase with education. Apparently, those with a college degree are more likely to express confidence in paranormal ability that those with less education.[91] This is even more surprising when we consider that only a small number of those polled—16%—say they actually had a personal encounter with paranormal activity, such as the reading of a psychic or medium. So even though most people have never met a psychic, their faith that some individuals can have extrasensory communications is still strong.

Needless to say, these results have failed to sway scientists. A survey held among members of the National Academy of Sciences revealed that only 10% expressed an interest in conducting research on people with paranormal gifts. [92]

That doesn't take away the fact that some scientists have been fascinated by the abilities of both psychics and mediums. The essential difference between the two is that mediums are people who are able to communicate with the spirits of the dead, whereas a psychic is a person who can perceive, and interact with, a far broader range of spiritual information. That includes not only spirits of the dead, but also spirits—or energies—that attend us in daily life, both within us and in the environment in which we live. Parapsychologists identify four areas in which a psychic can have such extraordinary abilities. These are (1) *Clairvoyance*, the ability to perceive things from the past, present or future outside of normal human contact; (2) *Telepathy*, the ability to transmit or receive information outside of normal human contact; (3) *Precognition*, the anticipation of an event before it occurs, and (4) *Psychokinesis*, the ability to move objects through a focused mental effort alone. Together, these four are known as *psi* phenomena. What makes this so interesting for the study of our consciousness is that, in Charles Tart's words, all four of these abilities "are manifestations of *mind* that have resisted all attempts to reduce them to known physical forces."[93] In other words, the mind of the psychic is *ipse facto* living evidence that our consciousness operates independently from the organic functioning of our brain, for the simple reason that *psi* phenomena are functions that no normal human brain can perform.

Famous Psychics

As we saw, ancient cultures had great respect for those able to see visions or receive prophecies. It is possible, for example, that some of the prophets of Hebrew Scripture had psychic ability. "Prophecy," says the Book of Numbers, is the gift of "one who hears the words of God, who has knowledge from the Most High, who sees a vision from the Almighty" (Numbers 24:16). The New Testament agrees. "Prophecy never had its origin in the human will," says the Second Letter of Peter, "but prophets, though human, spoke from God as they were carried along by the Holy Spirit" (2 Peter 1:21).

One famous example is the story of Joseph. According to the book of Genesis, Joseph rose to the position of Grand Vizier, an official with an authority second only to Pharaoh, because he could interpret dreams. In ancient times, an oracle—a person able to see and decipher dreams, or visions of the future—was a revered figure. While some believe the oracle of Delphi—a woman named the Pythia—was lured into a trance using drugs or herbal fumes, others argue that she may have been a psychic, chosen from a pool of women who possessed such exceptional abilities. Another famous prophet was the Frenchman Nostradamus, who in 1555 published a book called *Les Propheties* ("The Prophesies") that, many believe, predicted such modern calamities as the rise of Adolf Hitler and the 9/11 attacks.

During the 18th century era of the Enlightenment, another psychic who achieved great renown was a Swedish scientist named Emanuel Swedenborg, famous for discovering the neuron. After experiencing a spiritual awakening at age 53, he devoted the rest of his life to researching the spiritual world, which he documented in 28 books. One of these was a work called *Arcana Coelestia* or "Heavenly Mysteries," written in Latin (the universal language of scholars at the time), which argued that the true meaning of the Bible is to show the gradual transformation of humans from materialistic to spiritual beings.

On the evening of July 19, 1759, he happened to have dinner with friends in the city of Gothenburg, some 300 miles from Stockholm. At 6:00pm, he suddenly stood up and announced that a great fire had broken out in the Swedish capital. In his vision, he saw that the fire had destroyed the house of his neighbor and was now threatening his own. As his friends waited anxiously, he paced around the room until two hours later, he was relieved to report that the fire had spared his house. Many others in the city, he said, had been made homeless.

It was not until two days later that the first courier from Stockholm arrived in Gothenburg with news that a great fire had leveled much of the city. Later reports indicate that Swedenborg was entirely accurate about the timing: the fire had indeed broken out shortly before 6:00pm. Given the lack of instant communications in the 18th century, there is no explanation for how he was able to "see" the fire, except through communication with a spiritual source.[94]

Another influential author from this era was the German physicist Franz Mesmer, the first scientist to theorize that there must be a magnetic energy field (or *Lebensmagnetismus* as he called it) that operates both among and inside all living things, and even inanimate things. His theory, which today we would call the study of bio-energy, became known as mesmerism.[95] Rebuffed by his German colleagues, Mesmer moved to Vienna where he married a wealthy widow. This allowed him to deepen his studies while also serving as a patron of the arts. That is how a reference to Mesmer wound up in, of all places, Mozart's opera *Così fan tutte*. But a failed attempt to cure the blindness of a young piano player eventually compelled him to move to Paris.[96] Here, he further developed his ideas about a human source of inner energy that has much in common with Indian Chakra and Chinese Qi systems. He also treated a large number of patients with his spiritual gifts, news of which eventually reached the ear of King Louis XVI. The king was so intrigued that he appointed a special royal commission to investigate Mesmer's spiritual practice. One of its members was a man who was also interested in paranormal phenomena, though he served as American ambassador to the French court. His name was Benjamin Franklin.[97]

In America, the idea that spirits exist both on this earth as well as in the hereafter spawned a 19th century movement known as *Spiritualism*. Spiritualists believe not only that spirits operate on a higher cognitive level than humans, but that there are certain exceptionally gifted human beings who can communicate with these beings. Spirits are therefore privy to knowledge and information that could help humankind in its progress to a more advanced and just society. This is when the concept of a "spirit guide" first emerged: the idea that spirits are willing and ready to assist human beings—even average men and women without special psychic abilities—if only they would open themselves to such spiritual guidance. In other words, Spiritualists believe (as do many psychics today) that in principle, every human being has the capacity to perceive messages from spirit guides, if they are prepared to attune their mind to such a stimulus.

Spiritualism became so popular that just before the turn of the century, it was believed to have some 8 million adherents in the United States, as well as large numbers of followers in Great Britain and Continental Europe. For example, Arthur Conan Doyle, the author of the Sherlock Holmes detective novels, and fellow author Charles Dickens were devoted spiritualists. So was the famous French physicist and Nobel laureate Pierre Curie.

In America, early psychics included two ladies, Cora L.V. Scott and Achsa W. Sprague, whose carefully staged trances attracted huge audiences in the years before the Civil War. The subsequent success of the "Fox Sisters," who claimed to be in communication with spirits of the deceased, launched a veritable wave of clairvoyants and mediums. Before long, it became common to stage these séances as live entertainment, in theaters, before paying audiences. Inevitably, performers found themselves under pressure to make their shows ever more sensational, which soon led to accusations that these events were faked. In 1887, this prompted an investigation by the Seybert Commission, made up of faculty members of the University of Pennsylvania. The commission found that the industry of professional mediums was indeed tainted by widespread fraud.

You would think that these revelations did considerable damage to the credibility of the Spiritualist movement, but the opposite is true. The reason is the devastation left by the American Civil War, in which the Confederacy and the Union suffered a combined total of some 1.5 million casualties. That is a staggering number, keeping in mind that the population of America at that time was only 31 million—about a tenth of what it is today. Even worse is the fact that a decade after the end of the hostilities in 1865, some 400.000 soldiers were still unaccounted for. This prompted desperate wives, mothers and girlfriends to turn to mediums to find out if their loved ones were still alive. One of these was Mary Lincoln, the wife of President Abraham Lincoln, who insisted on having séances at the White House after the death of her son William in 1862.

That same desire spurred a new wave of interest in psychics after each of the world wars of the 20th century. While the numbers are not exact, historians generally agree that the toll of World War I amounted to 9 million soldiers and 12 million civilians killed— perhaps the first war in which civilian deaths exceeded the number of military dead by a wide margin. That trend continued with World War II, which led to the deaths of a staggering 75 million people in all theaters, or about 3% of the total world population. A full two-thirds of these victims were civilians, not soldiers, who died as a result of famine, bombardment, displacement, or the infamy of the Holocaust. The American armed forces alone lost 418,500 dead, including non-combatants such as nurses and rear-area staff, particularly during the Battle of the Bulge in late 1944. With 77,726 casualties, this battle ranks as the bloodiest engagement in American history.[98]

It is therefore not surprising that the American psychic Edgar Cayce found himself in great demand after the first American troops landed in Africa in 1942 and later in Europe, and anxious families contacted him for news about loved ones that were "missing in action." Cayce, one of the best-known American psychics, was born in Beverly, Kentucky in 1877. As a young child, he began to experience several paranormal visions, including one in which he met his deceased grandfather. He later described how at age 10 he was visited by a spirit in the form of a woman. She asked what he wanted to do with his life, and Cayce answered that he wished to be of service to those in need.

His biographer, Thomas Sugrue, tells a fascinating story of what happened when young Cayce entered first grade. Here, the young boy struggled mightily with spelling—so much so that he was in danger of falling behind in his class. His teacher mentioned this to Cayce's father, who flew into a rage. As soon as he got home, he subjected his son to a severe grilling about his spelling skills, and kicked the boy from his chair when it became clear that his writing was very poor. That is when Cayce heard the voice of the spirit he had encountered before. She told him to relax, and to take a brief rest. The boy promptly fell asleep on top of his grammar book. When shortly thereafter, his father returned to the room, Cayce woke up and was able to write flawless English, and complete all of the assignments in his text book.

In the years to come, Cayce found that this is how he could do all of his homework, simply by resting his head on the cover—which eventually gained him the epithet of "the sleeping prophet." It also inspired him as an adult to conduct a number of "readings" on a great variety of topics, including dreams, spirits, and relationships. In all of this, he stressed the vital link between health, exercise and meditation, thus becoming the first advocate of what today we would call a "holistic lifestyle."[99]

In 1941, after the attack on Pearl Harbor, Cayce was living in Virginia Beach, supporting himself with donations from his group of some 500 supporters. But as the American involvement in Europe grew, particularly following the D-Day invasion of June, 1944, he sometimes performed as many as eight readings per day, trying to determine the fate of soldiers missing in action. The experience drained him physically and emotionally, and he died in January of 1945.[100]

This desire to communicate with loved ones who have perished as a result of war continues to this day. Sue has spent many summers in Bosnia at the request of anxious mothers and wives, visiting the grounds of former Serbian concentration camps where Muslim boys and men were held and often killed. "Every time I go there," she says, "I see faces of the victims that still permeate the energy field of these places. And each time I relive some of the truly horrific things that went on there." Whenever she experiences these traumatized regions, she tries to clear the dark energy with light. "I don't know how else to explain it," she says, "but what I try to do is work with the spirits to clear the energy layers, and restore a sense of peace." But, she adds quickly, "I don't want you to think that energy fields are just repositories of pain and suffering. Far from it. Sometimes you pick up places where there's been a lot of elation and joy, and you feel the jubilation pouring into your heart."

"You see," she adds, "When somebody is a high conduit for that energy, it automatically has a ripple effect. It touches somebody else and starts passing on that internal alignment, almost as if you are recharging a battery. And when you feel that hot, positive energy, it wants go out and keep flowing, always flowing. I think that's why there were people like Jesus, the Gautama Buddha, or the Mahatma Gandhi, who emanated this incredible healing and loving energy that touched everyone who came into contact with them."

As a result of her growing international renown, Sue is now traveling around the world, trying to teach other cultures the incredible power of positive and spiritual energy. "I was invited to go to Bali, to speak at some very famous *ashrams* (Hindu retreats)," she says, "and I was in a panic. I didn't know how to talk to Hindus about Hindu spirituality, or to Muslims about Islam. And I said to myself, 'what on earth are you thinking? How can you possibly satisfy all these people's needs?' But without fail, something amazing happens when I get up and walk to the microphone. It is as if I'm suddenly filled with a new dimension. I open my mouth and out come these amazing ideas that I would never have thought of myself. Yes, I'm the one talking, but it is actually the spirits that are speaking through me. I know that's a bit difficult to accept for many people, but that is absolutely the truth. It is not my wisdom; it is the wisdom from that great information field that the spirits are linking me to. I am simply their vessel."

Wherever she goes, that spiritual dimension is never far away. "It's like the story of my trip to Scotland that I told you earlier," she says. "I'm driving along this country lane, and suddenly I get this information about this valley that lies just across the hill. And I am told I should visit it. It's not as if someone is actually whispering in my ear; it's just a thought that suddenly wells up inside of me. It is like an inner desire. You cannot put it out of your mind. It fills your whole body with its importance. And if you run away from it, it will just keep nagging at you. So I have learned to follow that feeling, whatever the spirits suggest I should do."

Those impulses have taken her all over the world, to Sri Lanka, to Kenya, and to Indonesia. Sometimes, when she gets an invitation to visit another faraway place, she wonders if she has the strength to do it. "And at times like that," Sue says," my daughter tells me, "Mom, you must go, because you know this helps people."

To me, these reports suggest that understanding the role of spirits—who they are, how they behave, and why they behave the way they do— is key to understanding the spiritual world in the afterlife: not only how it functions, but also how it is organized. That is why, based on everything that we have learned so far, I'd like to take you on a journey – an incredible journey to our true home, the spiritual universe, from whence we came and to which we shall return.

In this Hubble image of Nebula NGC 346, scores of infant stars are being born from gas clouds that are collapsing under gravitational pressure (*Courtesy NASA/ESA*).

6. A Journey through Heaven

What is heaven? Where is it, and how do we get there? To understand the answers to these questions, we must first let go of some of our most cherished assumptions. Here is one of them: the idea that *life*, our life on earth, is what it's all about. That it is the *norm*, the extent of our very being, from the moment we receive life in the womb to the moment that our body gives out and dies. That idea is so deeply embedded in our human-ness that we actually call the hereafter the "after-life," as if it were some sort of Coda, some Appendix to our glorious existence on this earth. And of course, life can be glorious. Especially in a First World nation such as ours, we have the opportunity to grow into adulthood, to lead a healthy life, to be educated, to find someone we love and cherish, and to live a long and fulfilling life. Although many of our fellow citizens, and particularly minority citizens, do not always share in the fruits of the richest nation on earth, it is undeniably true that it is a privilege to live in the 21st century, and in a country such as ours. This is particularly true for me, for I am a first-generation immigrant. I came to the United States on May 10, 1979, as a graduate student with nothing more than a suitcase full of dreams. And as some of my stories throughout this book have shown, I have been blessed with love, fulfilling work, and friends and family who have given my life meaning and purpose.

If you are lucky enough to have had a similar experience, then you know how difficult it is to imagine that life on earth is *not* what it's all about. Of course, it is a very important part of who we are, but it is not the "end-all" that we think it is. In fact, as we will see in this chapter, there was a you and me *before* we were born, and there will be a you and me *after* we pass from this life. Our life on this planet is, quite simply, an interlude. A very long and exciting interlude, perhaps, but just an interlude nonetheless, in what is a long series of wonderful, conscious experiences.

To show you this, I am going to take you on a journey. It will be a wild and exhilarating journey, and sometimes a bit of an intellectual roller-coaster, but I think it will "blow your mind," as we used to say in the 1970's.

Now, the best advice I can give you before we embark on this trip is to let the ideas and images flow, without immediately trying to understand or question them, as our mind wants us to do. We are children of the Age of Reason, which means that our ability to imagine things is limited by what our mind *allows* us to see and perceive. But to understand the operational model of the universe, we must be like children. We must open ourselves to visions that are unlike anything we have seen before.

To begin, let's imagine that we are in a starship that takes us far from earth and into the depths of inner space. Traveling at the speed of many thousands of lightyears per second, we catapult out of our galaxy, the Milky Way, and zoom through clouds of stellar constellations, each more rapturously beautiful than the last.

Using space as a metaphor for the afterlife is particularly useful for several reasons. One is its vastness. The universe is bigger than anything we can conceive of on earth. It is so big that from our earthly perspective, we can only see a small part of it. In fact, today we can see even less, with our naked eye, than our ancestors did many centuries ago. I got a glimpse of that idea when, as a young student, I backpacked through the Sinai desert. That was the summer of 1973, to be exact, when the Sinai peninsula was still in Israeli hands after the conquest of the Six Day War, and the Yom Kippur War lay just simmering on the horizon. The Sinai was still a very undeveloped region then, long before the 1979 peace treaty between Israel and Egypt restored the peninsula to Egypt, prompting a boom of luxury resorts in Sharm el-Sheikh and along the coast of the Gulf of Aqaba. And because so much was still *terra incognita* for tourists, I joined a group of backpackers, just like myself, and together we moved deep into its interior. Our destination was *Jebel Musa*, Arabic for "Mountain of Moses," which tradition has identified as the place where Moses received the Stone Tablets (and the Jewish Law) from God. We boarded a ramshackle bus from Dahab, filled to the rafters with Bedouin families, and eventually made it to a Bedouin encampment not far from St Catherine's monastery. This ancient Roman convent has marked the pilgrim's path to the summit of *Jebel Musa* since the days of Emperor Justinian.

Exhausted, we fell asleep in our sleeping bags as the sun slowly passed behind the mountain ranges, painting the sky in a riot of pastels. Like many pilgrims before us, our plan was to witness the sunrise from the top of the mountain. Knowing that it would take us three hours to climb the mountain from our base, we set an alarm clock for 3:00am. When, all too soon, that clock woke me up, I looked up and saw something I had never seen in my life: a firmament filled with stars as far as the eye could reach. Rather than the pinpricks we see at night today, these stars sparkled like diamonds strewn across the dark velvet of night—some so close I thought I could reach up and touch them. My companions and I just sat there, open-mouthed, trying to absorb the immense majesty of the spectacle above us. Most stunning of all, a bright white cleft ran straight across the sky, like a shimmering belt of light—our galaxy, the Milky Way, visible to the naked eye. It was a reminder that in ancient times, the desert at night was truly a place of tremendous awe and wonder—a canvas on which the forces of the divine became tangible for human eyes.

Since that day in the Sinai desert, now 45 years ago, modern astronomy and astrophysics have grown by leaps and bounds. In 1980, Carl Sagan produced the *Cosmos* TV series for PBS. Though an avowed agnostic, Sagan wrote that "the universe was not created for our race to thrive, but that we are a product of something much larger." That idea was captured, that same year, by the launch of the Hubble Space Telescope, which allowed us to see things that no human eye had ever observed. Among others, the giant telescope proved that our universe is expanding (known as the "Hubble Constant"), while showing that the rate of expansion is actually accelerating. It also made it possible for scientists to calculate that our universe is (only) 13.7 billion years old, starting with the so-called "Big Bang."

Hubble has revealed some other exciting things as well. It has given us convincing evidence that dark holes, the existence of which was first theorized in the 1960's, are actually quite common throughout the universe. Even more intriguing is the fact that there appears to be a deep and mysterious correlation between the mass of a black hole and its galaxy host. Black holes are rather scary things that defy the laws of nature, or so it seems. Around its rim, a spherical surface known as the "event horizon" marks the point where material is swallowed up, never to be seen or heard from again. In 1976, Stephen Hawking argued that black holes behave strangely in other ways as well: they can explode as a result of quantum effects, thus introducing an utterly random form of unpredictability to the universe. When they do, he said, any information that might have been sucked up inside the black hole would be forever lost. Many of his colleagues, particularly quantum physicists, loudly took him to task with that declaration, arguing that the universe can never "forget." The result is a fierce debate that continues to this day.

Peering deep into the infinite reaches of space, in 2015 the Hubble telescope found something else that stirred the world: it identified the farthest known galaxy in the universe, a constellation known by the prosaic name of GN-z11 in Ursula Major, currently at a distance of 32 billion light years from earth. And during Christmas of 2015, people around the world were stunned by Hubble's stirring image of the *Pillars of Stars,* which shows huge pillars of gases, each some five light-years tall. Lit by ultraviolet light, an untold number of stars are constantly being born amidst the safety of its gaseous folds.

So this is the first thing we must remember as we embark on our journey through space: real "death" doesn't exist in the universe. Instead, when aging stars explode in an agony of light, known as a "supernova," the residue of that energy in the form of atomic mass and chemical matter, simply become the building blocks of an entirely new form of life.

Pillars of Stars, a composite of images taken by the Hubble Telescope showing the birth of stars in the Eagle Nebula (M16, NGC 6611). Source: NASA.

The second thing we discover as we soar through the universe is that *time* no longer seems to matter. That's also a bit of a shock, because for us on earth, time is essential. Everything we do is governed by time. The reason is obvious: our existence as human beings is temporary. Therefore, we parse that existence very carefully in units of days, hours and minutes, to make sure that we make good use of our life "budget" before the clock runs out and our bodies die. But time is no longer relevant when that limitation doesn't exist. In a world where things are always changing, a quantitative measurement such as time simply loses its meaning. At the same time, questions such as "when did all this start?" become fairly irrelevant as well. And that's very important, because the same is true for the spiritual universe, as we will see.

Just as our ideas about death and time are no longer valid, we must also let go of another cherished idea: *place*. On earth, location is everything. We think of the place where we live as our *home*, just as we identify ourselves as citizens of the city, state and country where we live. And the reason is that our human consciousness is harnessed by our physical body. In other words, the actions that we take are entirely predicated by the location where our body finds itself at any given moment.

That is quite a remarkable thing, when you stop to think about it. Because the fact of the matter is, our *consciousness* can take us anywhere we want to be. We may not have the talent for out-of-body travel that psychics like Sue have, but we certainly have the capacity to take our mind off a boring meeting, or the ennui of waiting in an airport lounge. All we have to do is close our eyes and whisk ourselves to, say, the memory of our honeymoon on a beautiful beach in Hawaii. In our imagination, we can soar across the Alps or *schuss* down the powdery slopes of Aspen Valley. That, of course, is why meditation is so powerful, because meditation is simply a fancy word for taking our mind *off things* and allowing our imagination to roam free. And if you do that on a regular basis, you actually look forward to that time in the day when you can let your consciousness drift from your body, and experience the deep sense of rest and joy of an untethered mind.

Well, the same is true for deep space. Here, the idea of place is utterly pointless as well. And why is that? Because throughout human history, our science and sense of self have always been determined by our location: the planet earth, currently residing in a neighborhood known as the solar system. But what if that earth no longer existed? We could roam through the universe without any sense of direction, because our principal source of reference would be gone.

That also applies to the spiritual universe—the universe to which we will all return as spirits, after our bodies die. In other words, this is a domain where the three fundamental principles of life on earth—time, place, and permanent death—no longer rule. They have become meaningless. Instead, we will freely drift in a world without borders or walls, without the sense of day or night, and without the sense of time. Instead, all of our senses will be focused on our *being*. Our cognitive being. Our consciousness.

But what form does that consciousness take, you ask? When I die and enter this spirit world, what am I? Am I a spirit? A cloud of energy? A plasma field?

That is very difficult question for scientists to answer. In fact, it's even difficult for us, even though you, the reader, will by now have accepted the essential duality of who we are, as both mind and body, spirit and matter (or at least, I hope you have!). But what will spirits look like? What will *you* look like as a spirit? How do we recognize each other?

Sue told us how one night, her spirit guide manifested itself as a cloud of rainbow colors. As we saw, that's because the spirit felt Sue's resistance, her reluctance to embrace her talents as a psychic. And so the spirit guide showed itself in a way that could be "seen" by mortal eyes: as a spectrum of colored lights, alive and changing, so it could not be dismissed as a mere optical illusion.

Of course, in the heavenly realm that I am talking about—we will refer to it as the *spiritual universe*—spirits don't need to manifest themselves that way. They are energy, and as energy they can take any form, usually expressed as a function of light. Virtually every person who has had a near-death or regressive hypnotherapy experience talks about the Light. The light that beckons them to the portal, the light that guides them, the light that awaits them. "When I see the spirit," Sue says, "everything is pure light. That's the energy I see." And when she sat at the deathbed of a friend, she literally saw his spirit slowly disengage itself from his body, as a cloud of light, filled with a matrix of many beautiful colors.

The obvious conclusion, then, is that the spirit is an *essence* that inhabits a human body, but that survives that body's death in order to return to the spiritual universe from whence it came. The funny thing is that apparently, each spirit *is still recognizable* as the person they once were. That is the only way we can explain how, according to NDE and hypnotherapy reports, people past the threshold of death are often astounded to see relatives who passed away before them. Even though they no longer have a physical shape, they are still recognizable, in some way or form, as the person they were in life. That doesn't mean that they have to "look" exactly like that individual. As we saw, many patients "sensed" that a deceased relative was with them. Some referred to them as an angelic presence. But they still retained a semblance of who they were on earth.

This also explains why bona fide mediums and psychics can

make contact with these spirits, and communicate with them, even though spirits no longer have a voice box or a tongue to speak with. The reason is that this communication clearly unfolds on a different plain, well outside the five senses of the human body. And because they operate on a higher plain, spirits can interpret things that humans cannot. They can identify the forces of energy fields and decode the information stored within them. That's how Sue, traveling in her car on a road in Scotland, suddenly experienced an inner urge to pull over, leave her car, and climb a ridge in order to visit a valley that she didn't even know existed—and thus discovered a battlefield with an intense energy of unresolved trauma.

Why would spirits do that, you ask? Why would they want to interfere with our lives? The answer is, because they want to help human beings. Because in most cases, they have experienced mortal life themselves, but are now part of a much more superior, much more intelligent domain. That domain has given them knowledge that could be of tremendous benefit in solving some of the pressing problems we have on earth. Spirits are anxious to communicate these insights to us, and that explains the whole purpose of why the spiritual universe exists to begin with, as we will see in a moment.

Now, this is nothing new I am telling you. All you have to do is open any book of foundational epics, whether the Mahabharata, the Ramayana, Genesis, the Odyssey, the Shahnameh, or the Gospels, to discover that human beings have always been guided by spirit or spirits, in whatever form, throughout history.

The problem is that today, we are no longer looking for this type of inspiration as we did in the past. We think we no longer *need* it. After all, our basic material comforts—our home, our car, our 4K television, our refrigerator and smartphone—seem to have resolved pretty much all of the existential problems that humankind has struggled with since its inception. And because we no longer see the need, we have lost the art of *trusting* spirituality. I don't mean that in a religious sense, though certainly, many of us engage in some form of spirituality through religious worship. But in order to truly trust spirituality, we must have the courage to *surrender our entire being* to that spiritual feedback. We must literally open our minds to spiritual information, and that requires effort—even for someone like Sue, though she has gifts well beyond what most of us have. And because it requires an effort, most of us feel we neither have the time nor the inclination to do that. After all, why should we? We're well taken care of. We live a comfortable existence. And for many of us, the prospect of death is still far on the horizon.

So that makes it rather difficult for spirits in our day to have any meaningful impact on our lives. We are simply not attuned to their wavelength.

The other reason why it is so difficult for us to accept the presence of spirits is that we are afraid of them. "I sense a lot of fear in people," says Sue, "even when I'm asked to do a reading of a loved one who has passed away." People are scared of spirits, because spirits have been demonized in our popular culture as ghosts, as demons bent on tormenting us. "Horror films like *Poltergeist* have embedded this idea that spirits are fundamentally evil," she says. "That is so wrong. I have seen spirits, and believe me, they are the most beautiful things. It is never frightening."

Another reason why people are afraid of spirits is that our

mind simply cannot grasp it. As Eben Alexander writes in his book, "the physical brain only permits certain patterns of awareness to emerge."[101] In other words, the brain filters out the data that it thinks it can control. And that's not surprising. Our brain is the result of tens of thousands of years of evolution, during which humans developed the skills to survive in a world that was populated by mammals far more powerful than they were. As a result, the brain learned to prioritize information that is directly relevant to the fight or flight reflex. "Everything the mind perceives," says Sue, "first goes through the brain's memory bank to see if it correlates with any constructs of fear. So if you've been taught that ghosts are evil and the stuff of horror, then most likely your brain will induce a flight response. It will match these appearances with what you are *expecting* to see."

This is another area in which our age is fundamentally different. In previous periods in history, long before there were horror films and vampire books, people had a very different attitude towards spirits. The epics I just mentioned are full of spirit guides or angelic beings that reveal themselves to humans. The most common response is surprise, or awe; but never fear. Take the Book of Genesis, for example. When an angel appears to the young Hagar after she has been cast out in the desert by Abraham's wife, and asks what she is doing, Hagar doesn't start screaming as we might; she simply replies, "I'm running away from my mistress Sarai" (Genesis 16:8). When the God of Exodus tells the Israelites to move to the Promised Land, he assures them that "I am sending an angel ahead of you to guard you along the way and to bring you to the place I have prepared" (Exodus 23:20), which is the Bronze Age way of saying that "the force will be with you." The Israelites were overjoyed to have that spirit at the helm of their forces.

Only in the New Testament, in the story of the Annunciation, do we hear of someone being afraid of an angel. But of course, that person is Mary, who was probably only 13 or 14 years old at the time (the usual age at which girls began their menses, which made them suitable for marriage). Right away, the angel Gabriel rushed to put her at ease. "Do not be afraid," he said to her, "for you have found favor with God" (Luke 1:30). What these stories tell us is that for people in Antiquity, the idea of seeing angelic beings was not scary but actually quite plausible, and devoid of the negative connotation that we attach to spirit sightings today.

Perhaps the most startling thing that Sue has ever told me about spirits occurred during our very first conversation. We were sitting at the table, drinking tea, and she suddenly said, "Oh. I can see your spirit guides."

I nearly fell off my chair. "What?" I said. "Like, right now?"

"Oh yes," she said. "There's one on either side of you."

I sat there, speechless, which made her laugh. "There's nothing to be afraid of," she said. "They're always with you, to help you. You're probably not aware of it, but they are. Everyone has them. I just happened to see yours, just now."

"What do you mean?" I blurted out. "They're, like, guardian angels?"

"Yes," she said. "Sure. You could call them that."

And then she tilted her head, looked at me, and said, "You know, you really do have a very interesting set of guides, and I mean that in all honesty. You have a very defined purpose in all the things you do, all the books you write. And that sense of spirit, well, it comes from somewhere. It's you, of course; but the message that you want to bring to the world, to try to represent people's eyes and visions and a different perspective on things—well, that's exactly the sort of thing that our spirit guides want us to do."

And that got her to talk about other times when she saw spirits, particularly when people die. "There's this spectacular light show," she says. "I know that sounds strange or disrespectful, but it's really true. When I sit with a person on his deathbed, I've seen angels come. Sometimes they can ease it by appearing in the form that you are comfortable with, but their true form is always light. I love it when they all come because they have this big pulsing light with beautiful complex patterns that get really close—so close that you can feel their energy. When somebody dies, the whole room gathers with this light. I always feel so privileged to be able to witness that, even though it's sad to lose a friend." Andriana Eliadis believes there may be scientific evidence for the release of this light. A 1987 study found that at the point of death, the human brain appears to emit a measurable burst of electromagnetic energy.[102]

"What this means," Sue continues, "is that death is actually a joyful event. A person has had a long and full life, and now has fallen ill, and maybe suffering as a result. But there is a happy ending. The old body is discarded; it has fulfilled its role; and now the spirit is free once more. All the pain is gone, and in its place is nothing but light—gorgeous, beautiful light."

What the Spiritual Universe Looks Like

Which brings us back to our journey through the spiritual universe.

As we saw, unlike our physical universe it is a domain where space and time no longer exist. But what does this world look like? What do we see when we move through this spirit world? Do we find ourselves in outer space, or are we in a place similar to earth?

Here again, NDE and hypnotherapy reports can provide us with a fascinating glimpse of what we will see in this new domain. Many witnesses describe it as a world of stunning beauty, filled with dramatic landscapes, beautiful flowers, and gorgeous light. One witness named Arthur marveled at the superhuman vision he had suddenly developed. "The mountains appeared to be about 15 miles away," he wrote, "yet I could see individual flowers growing on their slopes. My vision was about one hundred times better than on earth." And he went on to say:

> "In the background were two beautiful, round-topped mountains, similar to Fujiyama in Japan. The tops were snowcapped, and the slopes were adorned with foliage of indescribable beauty... To the left was a shimmering lake containing a different kind of water—clear, golden, radiant and alluring. It seemed to be alive. The whole landscape was carpeted with grass so vivid, clear and green, that it defies description. To the right was a grove of large, luxuriant trees, composed of the same clear material that seemed to make up everything."[103]

A similar experience was related by a woman named Randi in 2004:

"There were thousands of colors in front of me. It looked like I was watching the Aurora Borealis. Then as if one of the rainbows of colors saw me, it came right at me and lifted me... I was watching the colors as I rode along the rainbow, and then, as if it was a wave, one of the colors hit me. I was immediately awash with an emotion, the emotion was the only emotion that I could feel, and then it was quickly replaced by another as I kept getting hit by the colors that were pure emotion.[104]

Another fascinating report was posted by Dan T. in 2003, who found himself in a lovely Italianate landscape. "It was really beautiful," he wrote later, "with gardens and fountains and small, countryside hills.

"The people appeared in Greek or Roman dress, very comfortable with white robes and sandal type shoes. A pocket of females was conversing near a majestic water fountain that also displayed Greek decor, with Seraphim, ivy and fruit. I didn't know what to do or say, so I just stood there and looked at them. A gorgeous blonde lifted her head my way and the others turned to greet me with very warm smiles. Then a man walking down a brick path to my left suddenly appeared waving his arms to the group of women calling to them, 'No! Do not speak to him, it is not his time.'"

These lyrical descriptions remind me of that wonderful movie with Robin Williams called *What Dreams May Come*, which in turn is based on a novel of the same name by the author Richard Matheson. In fact, Matheson once said that many of the visions in his novel were inspired by near-death experiences. In the film, Williams walks through fields filled with the most amazing colors, as if he suddenly found himself in a Monet painting.[105] This matches the description by an NDE witness called Lavette, who wrote that "I was amazed at how much more real and vibrant the colors and light around me were." Another witness wrote, "it was a beautiful land like no other I have ever seen in my life."

These visions suggest a few things. One, it is clear that in each case, the spirit found itself in an environment that was the epitome of natural beauty. Second, many of these pastoral descriptions match our idea of a primordial world: the state of earthly beauty before the onset of modern urbanization. There are few, if any, visions that involve modern skyscrapers, highways, or perhaps a *Blade Runner*-type futuristic city. Instead, the first encounter with the spiritual universe always seems to evoke a vision that corresponds to what we think of as the Garden of Eden. What does this mean?

One answer is that entry into heaven is mediated by certain sensations that are designed to be soothing, to put our spirit at ease while it is obviously going through a very traumatic transition. In that sense, the feeling of walking in a Garden of Eden can make us feel like we are back at the beginning, when the world was unspoiled and hardly touched by the hand of man. In other words, the purpose of these visions may be to calm us, and make us feel safe. The same concern to help us cope with our transition may explain why some witnesses are "welcomed" by relatives on the threshold of the gate of light, so as to assuage their fears and let them know that everything is all right.

If that is true, then it is possible that these nature visions are prompted to some extent by our *expectations* of what a beautiful, primordial world would look like. Now, that doesn't mean that these visions are merely a projection of our consciousness, and that they don't exist in the actual spiritual realm. But it does mean that if the spirit world wants to make us feel comfortable after passing the threshold of death, it could do so by conjuring images that we would instantly recognize as a paradise.

This may also explain another observation: while the general perception of an ideal world in NDE reports is remarkably consistent, the details of that world—in terms of specific landscape features, plants and flowers—are not. Again, these details can simply be suggested by our own expectations. The appearance of Greek-style figures in Dan's experience, for example, may have been prompted by Dan's knowledge of ancient literature, or perhaps his travels to Greece. This is speculation, of course, but I would find it eminently plausible that in our first encounter with the superior intelligence of the spiritual universe, our post-mortem consciousness would be soothed with impressions that we find pleasing and welcoming. This is, after all, our consciousness that we are talking about, which is the culmination of all the memories and experiences that we accumulated in life. Michael Newton agrees. "When the soul sees images in the spirit world which relate to places they have lived (in) or visited on Earth, there is a reason," he says, which is that "a benevolent spiritual force allows for terrestrial mirages to comfort us by their familiarity. Our planetary memories never die—they whisper forever into the soul-mind on the winds of mythical dreams."[106]

This reminds me of a famous scene near the end of the science-fiction classic *2001: A Space Odyssey*, when the character of Keir Dullea enters an alien realm. To make him comfortable, the aliens have recreated what they think is a typical home on earth, even though the props are mismatched: a Louis XV-style chair, for example, sits on top of a futuristic, back-lit floor. That same idea returns in the film *Contact*, where Jodie is reunited with her father-spirit on a carefully simulated beach, and in Steven Spielburg's *A.I.*, where the boy-character is allowed to spend one more day with his genetically recreated mother in a staged mock-up of their apartment. The comparison is apt, because in these movies the recreations are actually drawn from the memory bank of the character. According to Sue, this is what makes the spiritual universe such an exhilarating experience: we merely have to think of something in order to "experience" it.

Meeting Other Spirits

But how long do these paradise-like impressions last? Does the *What Dreams May Come*-type imagery change once we are "settled" in the spirit world? Do we move on to another experience, another sensation altogether? We can find the answer to that question from another source of evidence: the experience of psychics and mediums. After all, they *are* able to communicate with spirits who have been in the spiritual universe for a very long time. And the information they have gathered may surprise you.

There is indeed a "transitional period" in which the spirit

slowly learns to adapt to the spiritual universe, and gradually loses the need or the desire to see earthly visions. As we become more comfortable as spirits, earth-like "props" borne from our earthly memory will become less meaningful.

Instead, says Sue, we will be drawn to what makes the spirit world such an incredible place: through our engagement with other spirits. And this raises the question that almost everyone asks of a medium or a psychic, which is: "When I return to the spirit world, will I be able to see loved ones who have died before me? Will I be able to visit my parents or grandparents? Will I meet long-lost friends?" The answer is: yes, absolutely! And why not? Just like you, they have passed on from their experience on earth, and will be eager to see you and share their love for you once more.

"But," people invariably ask, "how will I be able to recognize them? There must be a billion spirits in that place! Is there like a directory or something? Or is there a reception desk who can help me find them?" All logical questions, of course. But they show that we are still thinking of the space-time paradigm on earth. There is no space-time paradigm in the spiritual universe, so you don't need to *find* your way to a loved one. Neither do we have physical bodies, so you don't have to worry about what they will look like, or if you will recognize them. We are all the stuff of energy. Therefore, all you have to do is *think* of them, and they are there. The boundaries of age, time and distance that we know on earth no longer exist. As spirits, there is no limit to what we can experience, or with whom. Some of us may even want to meet celebrities, or plan a visit with famous artists or composers. I already have my list! At the top—other than my dearly departed parents, of course—are Leonardo da Vinci, Johann Sebastian Bach and the French Impressionist painter Berthe Morisot, who was the subject of a film I directed many years ago. Of course, language is not a barrier either: as spirits, we can communicate our thoughts without the need for an interpreter.

You may also yearn to see a long-lost pet. Many years ago, my wife and I were deeply saddened by the loss of Dulce, our beautiful Labrador Retriever. She lived to the ripe old age of 14, and then peacefully passed away. Will she be there, wagging her spiritual tail? Of course she will! As we saw, animals are made of energy, just as we are; therefore, they too will be there, waiting for us. One NDE witness, Bryce Bond, wrote: "Racing toward me is a dog I once had, a black poodle named Pepe...He jumps into my arms, licking my face...I can smell him, feel him, hear his breathing and sense his great joy at being with me again."[107]

In heaven, everything is spirit, and everything is light. Physical travel no longer exists: you think of someone, and that someone, that spirit, will join you. I know that is hard to grasp for us, but that is the tremendous joy of being a spirit: you can be anywhere at any time, and with anyone you wish. And if there are spirits you'd rather not see—such as your ex!—that's fine too, though communicating with that spirit may help you to overcome your differences and become a better spirit in the process.

So what happens after the initial "introduction" period? As we slowly become accustomed to our new life in the spiritual universe, do we "advance" in any way? All the evidence suggests that this is indeed the case. We will continue to experience growth as spirits, just as we experienced growth as humans on earth. Several sources even suggest that as spirits we pass through different "levels" as our consciousness expands, but this analogy may be a bit misleading. The word "level" still suggests a particular location, when what we are actually doing is gaining a higher form of intelligence.

In fact, the idea of different levels in the afterlife has always been part of our view of heaven. In his *Divina Commedia*, the Italian poet Dante spoke of nine celestial levels by which heaven was organized. Each of these was a separate sphere, largely inspired by the ideas of the Roman geographer Ptolemy, which were still valid in 14th century Italy. Similarly, Buddhism suggests that there are ten levels to full enlightenment. And in the intertestamental writings, the prophet Enoch—traditionally the father of Noah— traveled through ten heavenly realms in his passage to God (2 Enoch 3:2-22:1). The purpose of these different realms is, of course, to prepare ourselves for the eventual encounter with God, and to ensure that we have gained the necessary wisdom to appreciate that divine encounter.

In the spiritual universe, something similar is taking place. "It is actually a very complex world," says Sue. "Just think of the tremendous complexity and the sheer sophistication of our physical universe. Well, that same artistry drives the forces that make up the spiritual universe."

But if there are different realms in the spirit world, how are they distinguished? Do we pass through them all? And how do we know that we've advanced from one to the next? The answer is that the spiritual universe is organized in a number of realms or peer groups, that each of these communities have a particular purpose, a unique agenda. As a spirit, you may be drawn to one or more of these groups in order to more fully realize your consciousness and learning. According to the case studies cited by Michael Newton, many patients become deeply attached to their community, which serves as their "spiritual family." This is where they find their home, their base.

Do you need to gain entry to these realms in some way? Do we have to earn our way in?

"Oh no," Sue replies, laughing, "that's a typical expectation we have in our life on earth, where everything is based on merit, and exclusivity. These are not some secret societies or private clubs that you have to apply for. Think of them as individual activity centers in what is essentially a very large resort. There are so many of these domains in the spirit world that you will always be fully engaged. The spirits once gave me a glimpse of that world, and it was so incredibly complex, so intricate, that it was difficult for me to grasp. But it was also very, very beautiful. I think that's the quality that will attract you to any of these domains: their immense beauty. Whenever I connect with the spirit of a deceased loved one, or whenever the spirits allow me into the spirit world, I sense this intense connection. It never fills me with worry; it fills me with peace, it fills me with joy. I never, ever, met a spirit who in some way exuded negative energy. When things come with integrity from the highest place, it's always beautiful, always."

There are many other questions that we could ask, such as, "What do I do in the spirit world? Am I even *supposed* to do something, or could I just hang out?" But the thing is, these questions are still prompted by our earthly obsession with a particular time and place, and our inability to see anything without a beginning and an end. For in the infinity of the spiritual world, there is no beginning and there is no end. There simply *is*, and just being there is a source of intense joy.

It also means that, as we saw earlier in this chapter, our life on earth is *not* the norm; our life as the spirit is the norm. We were spirit before we were born, and we return to spirit after we die. Being human is simply a temporary state that we are tasked with. And when that experience is done, we return to the mother ship, as it were, which is the spiritual universe.

The Life Force of the Spiritual Universe

So then, what is the point of it all, you ask? Why is our life as a spirit permanent, while our time as a human being is so short? And here we get to the purpose of heaven, and indeed the purpose of why there is this incredible organization behind the universe. I recognize that this is perhaps a flawed word, because "organization" conjures up the image of a group of people, sitting behind desks in a large mission control room, working hard at managing things. Of course, that is not how the spiritual universe operates. But the astonishing thing is this: what drives this world, and what gives purpose to our physical and spiritual universe, is *not* happenstance. It is not purely the accident of a chemical explosion at the beginning of time, as Big Bang theorists want us to believe. The true answer is that there is a higher intelligence behind all this.

It took me a while to grasp the enormity of this idea, because if it is true, it would at last resolve the centuries-old conflict between faith and science that has vexed humankind since the Age of Enlightenment. For people who underwent a near-death or regressive hypnotherapy experience, there is absolutely no question that a higher intelligence, a higher source, does exit. It is this life force that governs both the physical and the spiritual world in a way that keeps both deeply intertwined—as a perfect marriage of matter and energy. "The greatest joy of being in the spirit world," says Sue, "is to connect with the purest form of the life force." Many of us called that life force "God." As we will see, most of the world's religions traditions agree on that point.

But how does this central life force, this "creator" manifest itself? And here I want you to sit down and grab your seat, because this is the most beautiful thing of all. The principal engine, the central source that governs the spiritual universe, is nothing but *love*. Pure, simple, unadulterated love.

Now, I know that some of you may find this difficult to accept. After all, our modern world is governed by anything but love. Instead, it is ruled by violence, envy, and hatred of every kind. Just open up a newspaper, or watch the news, or visit some political blog. Every day we are inundated with messages of divisiveness and brutality. So what's love got to do with it?

And the answer is, that is precisely why the spiritual universe *is everything our earthly existence is not*. Because love is simply the highest, most perfect expression of our consciousness. It is the most positive force imaginable, because no one would want to hurt someone—or something—that she or he loves. And when you think of it, that is also true for our life on earth. We feel most fulfilled, most *human* when we know we are loved. Love is not only the essential mortar of the world we inhabit; it is also the purest life force of what makes the intelligent universe tick. Love is what motivates our desire to come together, to seek unity, to foster cohesiveness. It is the very antithesis of everything that has made our world so fraught with danger, with violence, and despair. It is, quite simply, the most powerful form of energy imaginable.

"And the reason," says Sue, "is that we are a part of an energy form that wants to be cohesive. The vast masses of energy and matter floating in our universe—they swirl and attract one another so that they can become cohesive, and create something new. The same is true for the spirit universe that drives the physical universe." It is love that allows Sue to clear certain places of their negative energy and replace it with something good, something positive. "I always try to compare it to music," she says. "What we try to do is create harmonics. Each spirit is like a musical piece. When you find the musical match, when you play the harmony together, it's wonderful. It is about the spiritual frequency. That's love."

And remember: almost all near-death experiences talk about this incredible feeling of love. "I saw a place full of love and peace," wrote a Spanish NDE witness named Alicia. "I was accompanied by Beings, despite not being able to see them... I felt in my mind that one of them was talking to me. It was in a masculine voice that was very sweet and soft, with lots of love."

"I experienced pure love," said a Swedisch NDE patient named George. "There was no guilt, shame, or compulsion. The only thing that existed was pure, complete, and unconditional love. The love was so good and had answers to everything so that I had no questions to wonder about. The happiness I felt was total. To have gotten to know this love is the greatest gift I have had in my life."

A Frenchwoman named Marie-Pierre said, "I felt an immense universal love and peace in me. I felt like being on a cloud, but also in the cloud and myself the cloud. I was filled with a happiness that is not known on this earth."[108]

The Purpose of Being Human

But this raises another question. If we are the product of a spirit world filled with love, then what is the point of being tasked to go to earth—or any other place in the universe, for that matter—and assume physical form? Why do we have to leave this wonderful abode, so filled with love and happiness, in order to slog our way through a mortal life as human beings, with all the problems and suffering that this might bring? What purpose is there for spirits to come to earth?

It's a very good question, and a very logical one. After all, the world can be a very scary place. I am not going to take political sides here, but you don't have to be affiliated with a political party to see that our nation has become more polarized and divided than ever before. The same goes for the European Union, where neo-populist movements are straining the European project at the seams. Not to speak of the growing oppression, and the rise of autocratic regimes, throughout Eastern Europe, the Middle East and Asia. It seems that humankind is regressing, rather than advancing, in its quest to improve the lives of everyone on the planet. And if that is the case, then what's the point of sending more spirits down to try to stem the decline? If that's supposed to be the purpose of our mission, it doesn't seem to be working very well.

But looks can be deceiving, says Harvard psychologist Steven Pinker. The reason is that our media, from *The New York Times* on down to the lowliest blog, know that bad news sells better than good news. It's in our nature to want to read about the misfortune of others, to go *tsk tsk* and think, "there but by the grace of God go I." But, says Pinker in his book *The Better Angels of our Nature*, let's look at the facts. True, in 2017, there were 12 wars being fought around the globe, while 10 percent of the world population still loved in extreme poverty. Plus, the world's superpowers are still bristling with more than 10,000 nuclear weapons. But 30 years ago, almost double the number of wars were raging—23—while no less than 37 percent of the world population lived in extreme poverty. Meanwhile, NATO and the Warsaw Pact had over 60,000 nuclear weapons between them. So while we are still experiencing difficult challenges, he says, we are better off than a generation ago.

Overall, the quality of life has improved as well. As I wrote in my book *The Story of Christianity,* at the beginning of the 19th century, during the Napoleonic Era, most people lived in ways that were not significantly different from the days of the Roman Empire, nearly two thousand years earlier. The horse was the primary mode of transportation. The principal source of illumination was the wax candle. Most of Europe's cities were dangerous at night, for they were plunged in darkness. Information was transmitted by hand-written mail, with transfer times measured in the distance a horse could travel in a day—usually between 15 and 20 miles. Seaborne traffic was dependent on favorable winds.[109]

By the end of the 19th century, all of these axioms of human activity had been transformed. Major cities were now lit at night by gaslight. For the first time in history, rail networks and the steam-driven locomotive made long-distance travel affordable for millions, allowing them to escape the confines of their village or township. At the same time, the steam-driven turbine transformed seagoing traffic. Despite the hardship of working in mills or factories (including the exploitation of child labor), the Industrial Revolution caused standards of living to rise after its long decline in the 18th century. The cost of food dropped because of improvements in production and transportation. By the second half of the 19th century, the type of endemic famine and malnutrition that had been the scourge of Europe had all been eradicated. Vastly improved educational opportunities in the Victorian Era produced a new middle class of professionals, doctors and lawyers, as well as entrepreneurs, shopkeepers and artisans. Literacy rates rose from 15% to 72%. Today, over 90% of the world population can read and write.

As Pinker puts it in a Ted talk, "Progress does not mean that everything becomes better for everyone everywhere all the time. That would be a miracle, and progress is not a miracle, but a process of problem-solving." And when that, Pinker hit the nail on the head. Progress, and the moral advancement of humankind, is not a linear process. It has bursts of tremendous creative growth, such as during the Renaissance; and then suffers major setbacks, such as during the Thirty Years War, when 30% of the population of Central Europe died. "Human learning and progress comes in cycles," Sue says, "and each of these are big gateways for experience."

In *2010: A Space Odyssey*, the sequel to the original movie, the spirit of David Bowman contacts Dr. Heywood Floyd and tells him, "You see, it's all very clear to me now. The whole thing. It's wonderful." I think that this line says it all. The answer to the perennial question of "Why are we here?" is this: it is the *experience* of being human. To cope with the joys and challenges of physical life. To make decisions to the best of our ability. To try to live a good and moral life. And to learn from that process, so that when our spirit returns to the spiritual universe, we are no longer the same as we were before.

"You have to understand," says Sue, "that the critical factor here is *free choice*. Because we are endowed with free choice, our spirit gets caught up in the human drama, and has to make choices. How does that play out? That's where our energy, and the energy fields around us, start to pay attention." She smiles, and says, "You know, I've had huge lessons from spirits about how that free choice, of how we handle things in life, really makes a big difference to the collective energy. And you know, when you're in a debate with spirits, they don't just give you a straight answer. They want you to really explore it, and ask more questions. That process has helped me to fundamentally change my perception about good and evil in this world."

Perhaps we could summarize it in this way: the purpose of our time on earth is to have the opportunity to experience an incredible variety of emotions that we could never have in heaven. To taste happiness and despair, sadness and joy, fulfillment and disappointment, with an intensity that could only be experienced in the physical world. And to make choices as a result of those moments. That process enriches us as spirits. It can make us kinder and wiser, or it can make us scornful and bitter. But whatever it is—that's the experience that we carry back to the spiritual universe.

Remember how many NDE witnesses talked about their "life review?" One patient from South Africa, Victor Philip, remembered that "the light communicated telepathically with me. It was so natural. We discussed my life, and I relived portions of it. We reviewed my life from the oldest to most recent events, and only stopped when I seem to be uncertain of my own actions at the time. There was no condemnation and no right or wrong. There was complete acceptance and understanding, with only one loving comment, 'Don't you think you could have done it this way?'"[110]

Of the countless patients that Newton treated with regressive hypnotherapy, there was not a single patient "who did not have a personal guide." It is by virtue of these guides that "we become more acutely aware of the continuity of life and our identity as a soul.... They are part of the fulfillment of our destiny."[111]

This is a continuous theme in all descriptions of a "life review": the spirit is encouraged to talk about choices made during its lifetime, but not for the purpose of facing judgment. My team and I have reviewed many hundreds of NDE testimonials, and in every life review, the witness never felt being put "on the spot," or forced to incur punishment for something done wrong. In each instance, the purpose of the review was simply to assess whether the spirit *understood* the moral ramifications of its actions.

"I was able to re-experience all these events in my life," wrote one NDE witness named Karen, "but just as importantly, I was able to experience the impact of my actions and words on those other people with whom I had interacted. Not one of the spirits condemned me for those painful things I had done or not done, but I felt so very sorry and sad about them within my own heart. It all seemed to happen very quickly, but had a tremendous impact on me. I got the impression that these spirit beings had been with me and had helped me plan my life before I was born. They let me know that I would be able to return to my life, if I chose to do so."[112]

Another NDE witness, Katherine, had a very similar experience after suffering catastrophic blood loss during laparoscopic surgery. "I communicated with [the spirits] about my decisions during my life review and areas where I could improve," she remembered. "While it was a collaborative process, I had deep respect and reverence for these beings. I felt that they loved me completely and without any judgment. In psychology there's a term called 'unconditional positive regard.' I felt completely sure that they had this feeling for me. It felt like a warm glow of light around me. The conclusion of these conversations was that it wasn't so much a decision of doing the 'wrong' thing in situations, or making unwise choices, but that the times of greatest challenge for me were times in which I could have acted but chose inaction." In other words, the things we do on earth have consequences when we return to the spiritual universe. That certainly applies to our own transgressions, of things we've done that hurt the people around us, but it also applies to people who have committed horrible crimes, who have raped or murdered other human beings and caused intense suffering. The question I am often asked is, would Hitler be allowed into this spiritual universe? What about Stalin or Genghis Khan? If this realm is so suffused of heavenly love, then why is there so much violence and evil on earth? How could a merciful God allow things like the Holocaust, or genocide?

The answer is that only the presence of evil can help us understand the cardinal virtues of mercy and compassion. Without it, the quintessential role of free will would have no purpose. The purpose of the life review, then, is to compel spirits who lived unethical lives or committed evil to account for themselves. Newton believes that our deeds on earth directly determine our "karma" in heaven. Karma is a Sanskrit word that literally means "deed" but actually refers to the consequences of our actions: a good life produces good karma; a life of evil produces bad karma. In his view, "perpetrators of harm to others will do penance by setting themselves up as future victims" once they are reborn in another persona on earth.[113] Another way of looking at it is to imagine that we must acknowledge the poor choices we made during our time on earth, and demonstrate our ability to learn from them. That is the whole purpose of the "debriefing" that many patients describe upon their entry into the spiritual universe.

And what happens when we finish our life review, and have reflected on our choices in life? Are we allowed to go out and play? Well, certainly. We can relax and bask in the glow of love that fills the spirit world. We can meet with whomever we want. Or we can simply revel in being ourselves, our consciousness, without any of the constant demands that were made on us back on earth—in our careers, our family responsibilities, or simply the daily labor of makingbe ends meet.

Most importantly, we can make good use of everything we have learned. We can "tap into" the great data bank of the spiritual universe and learn from the experience of others. We can "rewind" history and see where humankind went off the rails, where leaders made bad decisions, or where we failed to properly respond to great disasters such as famine, or floods, or the outbreak of war. And then, when we are ready, we can take on the task of serving as a spirit guide ourselves. We can devote ourselves to the wellbeing of someone else who is just about to born on the good planet earth—or any other planet in the universe.

Meeting God?

Yes, I know that at this point you have to pause for a second, and spend some time to absorb these ideas. It does seem a bit like science fiction, doesn't it? Or perhaps you're reminded of that great movie, *Defending Your Life*, where perfect human beings like Meryl Streep get five-star accommodations, while selfish slobs like Albert Brooks are dropped at the local motel to await their "life trial." Could it be that simple? Could there really be such a grand scheme that drives our humble lives? Is there truly some vast intelligence, called God, that governs everything in the universe?

And my answer to that is, "why not?" Have we all become such cynics that we can no longer believe in the idea of a higher, moral being? Everything we have covered in this book can lead us to only one conclusion: that spirits are a fundamentally benign force who are trying to make the *other* world, the physical world, a reflection of the intense love and beauty of heaven. "I was enveloped in a love I could not put into words," a patient called Helen remembered. "This divine love was in everything, as well as in me. At the core of my being, I was this love and so was everyone else." [114] A young woman named Laurie, who drowned and was later resuscitated, said that "I looked up and saw a huge ball of light that cast the purest, warm light all around me, and I felt God touch my skin. He knew me, and he loved me no matter how imperfect my Earthly life had been."

For these witnesses, God was revealed as the driving source of energy that animates all life, in both the spiritual and physical universe. That Source is what inspires us to learn and grow in our journey as spirits. It is obviously not a person, no matter how much we may admire Michelangelo's depiction of God in the *Creation of Adam* on the ceiling of the Sistine Chapel. In other words, it is not an anthropomorphic entity, even though humankind has always depicted its gods as human beings, for the simple reason that our minds can't imagine God in any other form. But this God must be an intelligence so superior and advanced that our consciousness may never be able to grasp it. That is why God makes himself felt in a way that everyone understands—through love.

As we come to the end of this chapter, I hope you have enjoyed this tour of heaven. But I sense that some of you are still skeptical. You may be thinking, "Well, this all sounds great, but where is the evidence for all this? Are we supposed to accept this at face value? Where is the proof?"

And I don't blame you. For a long time, I was like you—a scholar who believed that every claim should be backed by hard, physical evidence. That is why I began this book by introducing a number of relatively simple ideas, each of which attests to a simple truth: that human beings are made of two very different dimensions: matter and spirit. And if we are prepared to accept that, then it follows that the death of one of these—our body—doesn't necessarily involve the death of the other—namely, the spirit. Everything that I have showed you flows from the fundamental idea of a dualistic existence.

Of course, you don't have to take my word for it. In fact, the real evidence, the *hard* evidence, can only be found in—yourself. That divine spark, that spirit that we have been talking about, lives in yourself. All you have to do is find the right wavelength to not only identify it, but also communicate with it.

Yes, that takes some effort. Most of us, myself included, have been tone-deaf to what our spirit has been trying to tell us for much of our lives. We think we're too busy trying to stay on top of things, every waking moment of the day, to bother with such fuzzy notions as spirit and energy. No one can expect you to suddenly being able to "tune in" and hear what the spirit is telling you. But let's say that, from here on forward, you do want to find the spirit within you. How do you do that?

You do that by taking yourself away from your daily chores, and try to find time for "mindfulness," for prayer and contemplation. That is why in centuries past, people used to go on pilgrimage. A pilgrimage center such as Santiago de Compostela, in Northern Spain, would draw hundreds of thousands of pilgrims during specific seasons in the liturgical year. While the Jerusalem Temple still stood, Jews from across Israel and the Diaspora would converge on Temple Mount in Jerusalem for worship during three major festivals: Passover or *Pesach*, "Weeks" or Pentecost (*Shavuot*), and the festival of "Booths" (*Sukkot*). These festivals are still celebrated today, but at home or in the synagogue, because the Temple no longer exists.

Today, the only major faith that still has a scheduled annual pilgrimage is, of course, Islam. Each year, during the twelfth lunar month known as *Dhu al-Hijjah*, Muslims from around the world travel to the Hejaz in Saudi Arabia for the pilgrimage or *hajj* to Mecca. There they spend a week in prayer, while walking certain prescribed routes.

These and other routines all have one major purpose: to compel us to set our material concerns aside, so that we can surrender ourselves wholeheartedly to find the spirit within us. And this brings us to the next question: if this is how the spiritual universe operates, how does that compare to our religious beliefs about the afterlife?

Young worshippers at a temple near Tampaksiring, Bali

7. The Spiritual Universe and Our Religious Beliefs

Today, the only people who still talk about the afterlife on a regular basis are our clergy. It is during sermons on our holy day—*Jumu'ah* or Friday prayers for Muslims, *Shabbat* on Saturday for Jews, Sunday worship for Christians—that we might still hear about the promise of life after death. As a result, it is these theological concepts that have shaped our thinking when we imagine the afterlife.

The problem is that these ideas vary greatly among the three monotheistic faiths. In fact, while these traditions have much in common, it is in their concept of the afterlife that we see some significant differences. That made me wonder: if our concept of the spiritual universe as described in the previous chapter is correct, then how does this compare to our idea of heaven, *Jannah*, *She'ol*, or *Nirvana*?

To answer this question is trickier than you might think, because throughout history Jewish and Christian sages have never quite agreed on what form the afterlife would take. Therefore, as we saw in the Introduction, there is no clear and succinct description of the Christian heaven or the Jewish *Olam Ha-Ba*, the "World to Come," in contrast to the wealth of material that exists about the Muslim *Jannah*. That's perhaps not surprising when you consider that the three Abrahamaic faiths originated in very different periods of time. Judaism was born in the highlands of Canaan, sometime in the 10th century B.C., when much of the region was dominated by Syrian and Egyptian culture. Christianity only came about a thousand years later, when that same region— now called Judea—was ruled by Greek and Roman ideas about God and the afterlife. And Islam emerged another six centuries after that, when the Arabian peninsula was governed by a variety of local pagan practices, with Jewish and Byzantine influences percolating along its fringes.

The Afterlife in Islam

As a result, I always find it striking that of all three religions, Islam has a very concrete idea of what life after death will be like. For Muslims, Paradise or *Jannah* is a return to the primordial garden where Adam and Eve dwelled before they were seduced by Satan, and ate from the tree of immortality (Qur'an 7:21). Indeed, one Islamic tradition suggests that Paradise was not located on earth but in heaven, so that when Adam was expelled by God from Paradise, he literally *fell* to earth – and landed on the spot that is today is marked by the Dome of the Rock in Jerusalem. Another tradition has Adam descending to India, while Eve is sent down to Jeddah. Eventually, they make their way to Mecca, where they are finally reunited.[115]

Paradise is a lush place, says the Qur'an, for "beneath it flow rivers. Perpetual is the fruits thereof and the shade therein" (Qur'an 13:35). It is, however, a place to which admission is by no means guaranteed. According to Muslim *Tafsir* writings (the Muslim equivalent of the Jewish Talmud), believers have to *earn* their return to the Garden of Eden, by leading an exemplary and moral life. According to one account, Muhammad said that "it is paradise that God promised for His faithful after life for their deeds."[116] The Qur'an is even more specific, and states that paradise is only reserved for those who

> "....spend their days (benevolently) in ease as well as in straightness, and those who restrain (their) anger and pardon men; and God loves the doers of good (to others)" (Qur'an 3:134-6).

So what is this paradise like? The *Tafsir* literature describes it as a place full of wonderful, physical pleasures, "as vast as the heavens and the earth." For example, regardless of their age at death, all men and women will be 32 years old– the same age as Jesus upon his Ascension. Men and women will be clothed in gorgeous garments adorned with previous jewels. Banquets will be served around the clock, served by beautiful youths, and enjoyed in the company of loved ones – provided they, too, have led an exemplary life. "They will eat delicious food and drink," says the Qur'an, "and every bowl will have a new taste." And, the book continues, "We shall mate [the believers] with companions pure, most beautiful of eye" (Q 52:20, 55:56-58).

These are the famous "beautiful companions" (*Houri*), of "modest gaze," that some Hadith refer to as the seventy-two "wives" or "virgins."[117] Other Hadith claim that all women, regardless of age, will simply be restored to their prime of youth and beauty. "Lo!", says one, "We have created them a (new) creation and made them virgins, lovers, equal in age."[118]

From the Islamic perspective, then, the afterlife is an unending experience of pure pleasure, where "one day in paradise is equal to a thousand years on earth." That pleasure is made even greater by the joy of being close to Allah, to God. It is, however, only available to Muslims, and only those Muslims who lived a devout and morally upstanding life. While some *suras* (Quranic chapters) suggest that Jews and Christians, "those who believed in Allah and the Last Day and did righteousness," will have "their reward with their Lord," that tolerance does not extend to an admission into the Muslim paradise.[119]

But what will happen to sinners in Islam? They will be condemned to *Jahannam*, a word that is closely related to *Gehennom* in Hebrew and is usually translated as "hell." This is a very uncomfortable place with seven different levels of punishment, the worst of which feature torments such as fire (*Al-nar*) and boiling water. Evildoers are committed to any of these levels depending on the seriousness of their transgressions. The Qur'an has as many as 77 references to *Jahannam* that describe its torments in great physical detail—obviously as a direct counterpoint to the physical pleasures of *Jannah*. So, for example, will your body be scorched by fire, only to grow new skin so that the torment can begin anew (Qur'an 4:56).

The Jewish Afterlife

By contrast, Judaism is very ambiguous about the possibility of an afterlife. In Hebrew Scripture (or what Christians call the "Old Testament"), there are only oblique references to a life after death, as in the Book of Isaiah: "But your dead will live; their bodies will rise."[120] After warning that rich people, notwithstanding their wealth, "will perish in their grave, far from their princely mansions," the author of Psalm 49 adds, "'God will redeem me from the realm of the dead; he will surely take me to himself.'"[121] The psalmist uses the Hebrew word *she'ol* for "realm of the dead." In ancient Judaism, this was believed to be a rather grim place, where the souls of the deceased dwelled in limbo. These souls were literally the shades (*rephaim*) of their former self, brought together in a dark and forbidding place without any regard for their deeds in life, righteous or not.

It is only in later centuries, partly under influence from Greco-Roman culture, that the Jewish literature began to address questions of paradise (*Gan Eden* or "Garden of Eden") and *Gehennom* or "hell." In Greek mythology, for example, the underworld is called Hades, an underworld that lay just beyond the river Styx in the depths of the earth. That is why a bereaved family would always place a coin on the tongue of the deceased, so that the soul could pay a ferryman called Charon to take him across the river. And there, the souls would remain forever, as a shade of one's former self, bereft of strength (*menos*) or intellect (*phrenes*).

There was an exception, though, and that was the Elysian Fields, also known as Elysium. This was believed to be a truly beautiful place. Here, "the happy souls reside," wrote Virgil in his *Aeneid*; "In groves we live, and lie on mossy beds."[122] In Elysium, Homer wrote, "life is easiest for men. No snow is there, nor heavy storm, nor ever rain."[123] As Dante wrote in his Divine Comedy, Elysium is truly a "place for the blessed."[124]

The only problem was, Elysium was reserved for the gods, and perhaps a few mortals and heroes that they favored above all others. Less fortunate souls who did not enjoy the favor of the gods, including most common men and women, wound up in a place called Asphodel Meadows. Here the appointments were comfortable but, let us say, three-star at best. The truly wicked, meanwhile, were condemned to a forbidding place called Tartarus, a deep abyss filled with torment from which no soul can escape.

Under the influence of these ideas, Jewish attitudes towards heaven began to change as well. The Book of Daniel, which probably reached its final form in the 2nd century B.C., speaks of a Resurrection of the Dead, when "many of those who sleep in the dust of the earth shall awake, some to everlasting life, and some to shame and everlasting contempt" (Daniel 12:2). This is perhaps the most explicit reference in Hebrew Scripture to the idea of an afterlife, although its date and origin suggests that the text may reflect both Greek and Persian ideas on the subject. When exactly this resurrection would take place is not always clear, though many sages believed it would occur during the messianic age, when the Messiah would come to restore Israel as a nation under God.

You may find this surprising, but the whole debate about whether a human soul is immortal or not was actually initiated by the Pharisees in the century before the birth of Jesus. The texts of the Talmud move this idea further by debating what kind of experience our souls would have in the *Olam Ha-Ba*, the World to Come. Some references suggest that our spiritual joy would be derived from studying the Torah (the first five books of Hebrew Scripture), while others believe that the pleasures would be more tangible, such as the enjoyment of banquets and sex not unlike the joys of the Muslim *Jannah*.

At the same time, the idea of a split between heaven and hell became more pronounced as well. Already, the founder of Rabbinic Judaism, Yohanan den Zakkai, had written in the late 1st century A.D. that there are "two paths before me, one leading to Gan Eden and the other to Gehinnom" (Berakhot 28b). The 3rd century Jewish collection known as the *Mishnah* teaches that "this world is like a lobby before the *Olam Ha-Ba*. Prepare yourself in the lobby so that you may enter the banquet hall." The 12th century Jewish philosopher Maimonides took this one step further, and wrote that the souls of all the righteous would eventually enjoy eternal rest in the presence of God—a concept that many Orthodox Jews still believe today. But many Reform rabbis have different ideas. As the renowned Judaica professor A. J. Levine once remarked, "Jewish beliefs in the afterlife are as diverse as Judaism itself, from the traditional view expecting the unity of flesh and spirit in a resurrected body, to the idea that we live on in our children and grandchildren, to a sense of heaven (perhaps with lox and bagels rather than harps and haloes)."[125]

We can therefore conclude that of all the three Abrahamaic faiths, modern Judaism has the least definitive idea of whether the afterlife exists, and in what form. Many rabbis are more concerned with how we live life, rather than with whatever may come after death.

The Christian Afterlife

Compared to these concepts, the Christian idea of heaven is very different from either Muslim or Jewish models. The theme of the Kingdom of Heaven as a reward for the faithful is a core principle of Christian theology.

The Early Christians certainly thought so. As a biblical historian, I have often written about the genesis of Christianity—not only to try to reconstruct the evolution of Jesus' life, but also to understand the very unique conditions in which Jesus found himself at the dawn of Rome's Imperial period. And for me, what is so astonishing about Jesus and his ministry is not that he could heal the sick and the lame, but that he introduced us to this intriguing concept of heaven—a *kingdom* of heaven, "as above so below" (Matthew 6:10). A place where we would go after we completed our journey on earth. A place where we would be united with all the loved ones who have gone before us.

In 1st century Roman Judea, the idea of such an afterlife was far more radical than many of us realize. Jesus was raised in an observant Jewish family, and ancient Judaism did not have a clear sense of what happens after we die. Similarly, most people in the Roman Empire believed that after they died they would simply live as shadows in Hades, without any of the joys of life on earth or the Elysian Fields. So imagine, for a moment, the impact of Jesus telling his Jewish and Gentile followers that the heavenly Elysium is *not* just for the heroes and the favored; it is, quite literally, for *all*. That news must have hit like a bombshell. An Elysium for everyday folks like me, rather than an club for the elite? But would there be enough room for all of us? Yes, said Jesus, explaining that in "my Father's house" there are "many dwelling places," so no need to worry about finding space. And he added, "If it were not so, would I have told you that I go to prepare a place for you?"[126]

As we saw, it was the Pharisees who first introduced the idea of the immortality of the soul during the Second Temple Period. In the Gospels and particularly the Gospel of Mark, the Pharisees are often portrayed as the antagonists of Jesus. Some passages even suggest that they were part of a conspiracy to kill him. But this is probably the result of the times in which the evangelists produced their Gospels. Mark, for example, wrote after the outbreak of the Jewish War in Judea in 66 C.E., when Jewish factions (not only the Zealots but also the Sadducees and the Pharisees) were roundly condemned as rebels in Rome and beyond. His Gospel, which is the oldest, was then largely incorporated in the subsequent Gospels of Matthew, Luke and John. In these Gospels, the antagonism between Jesus and the Pharisees (and other Jewish factions) is even more pronounced.

And yet, when you look closer, there appears to be a lot of affinity between Jesus and the Pharisees. The sharp debates on Sabbath observance and ritual purity, which Mark portrays as a conflict between Jesus and the Pharisees, were actually the type of disputes that the Pharisees enjoyed *amongst themselves.* Questions such as tithing, marriage, divorce, and caring for the sick—themes that return in many of Jesus' teachings—were also the subject of discussion among the Pharisees, which later become known as the Oral Law, and the Mishnah. When seen in this light, the Pharisees may have solicited Jesus' opinion because they believed his ideas had merit, and deserved consideration.[127]

That also includes favorite Pharisaic topics such as the resurrection of the dead and the immortality of the soul. There is a key difference, however: for Jesus, the idea of heaven had a very particular purpose. While it is often forgotten in today's political debates, Jesus was deeply concerned with the social injustice in his native Galilee. His teachings about the earthly Kingdom of God envisioned a world ruled by love, justice, and faith in God, as a reflection of the "Kingdom of Heaven." The "love" of his teachings was not romantic love but *agapè,* a deep compassion for the less fortunate among us.

As the Jesus movement changed from a "prophetic reform movement" within Judaism to a religious missionary movement within the Greco-Roman world, something important happened.[128] The survival of the soul now became a moral imperative, for it offered salvation in heaven to all.

This is the message that Paul brought to the Gentiles; in his first letter to the Thessalonians, he wrote: "For the Lord himself ... will descend from heaven, and the dead in Christ will rise first. Then we who are alive, who are left, will be caught up in the clouds together with them to meet the Lord in the air; and so we will be with the Lord forever" (1 Thessalonians 4:16-18).

Punishment in Hell

As in Islam and Judaism, there is a counterpoint to the Christian view of heaven, and that is that unrepentant sinners will be damned to hell. "To die in mortal sin without repenting and accepting God's merciful love," the Catholic Catechism says, "means remaining separated from him forever by our own free choice." The Gospels refer to hell with the Greek word *Gehenna,* which is once again rooted in the Hebrew word *Gehennom.* In the 7th century B.C., the Valley of Hinnom near Jerusalem was sometimes used for child sacrifice as part of the cult of Moloch (2 Kings 23:10). The valley soon thereafter became synonymous with "hell." "It is better for you that one of the parts of your body perish," says Matthew, "than for your whole body to be thrown into Gehenna" (Matthew 5:29).

Throughout the Middle Ages and the early Renaissance, the presumed torments of hell were a favorite subject for painters such as Hieronymus Bosch. But today, not many Christian pastors still cling to the idea of hell as a separate place of eternal damnation and torture. Whereas in 1908, Pope Pius X still described hell as a "state to which the wicked are condemned, and in which they are deprived of the sight of God for all eternity, and are in dreadful torments," a century later Pope Benedict XVI presented hell as simply a condition in which the chief punishment is eternal separation from God. In other words, it is a state of being, rather than a specific location, though some evangelical leaders still adhere to the idea of hell as a place of eternal punishment.[129] In addition, modern theologians point out that the purpose of hell may simply be to motivate God's gift of free will. What would be the point of a free will, they ask, if all human beings wound up in heaven by default, regardless of the quality of their life on earth? It is the prospect of hell, of being denied God's love, that makes the choices we make morally tangible and relevant.

Similarly, there is no agreement among Christian denominations today whether souls are admitted into heaven immediately upon death, or only at the Day of the Last Judgment, at the End of Times. Thomas Aquinas, a 13th century Scholastic theologian, believed that "as soon as the soul is set free from the body it is either plunged into hell or soars to heaven," but that is not held by many evangelicals, who believe that the afterlife may unfold in separate phases.

Regardless of the process of admission, one thing we do know is that the Christian heaven is not the material, pleasure-filled resort envisioned by Islamic writings, and even by some Talmudic texts. Instead, heaven is a spiritual domain where souls experience the joy of love with one another in close proximity to God. During the Baroque era, the artists of the Counter-Reformation tried to make that world tangible. Fully aware that Calvinist and Reformed churches prohibited any form of sacred imagery, these painters gave us amazing, cinemascope views of heaven on countless church ceilings throughout Italy, Spain, Austria and Germany. In these visions, the deceased appear in the full glory of their human form amongst the clouds, dressed in magnificent robes while enjoying the attentions of attractive angel-maidens and adorable little *putti*.

Agreement Among the Faiths

Both the Jewish, Christian, and Muslim ideas of heaven revolve around the idea of proximity to God. It is the joy of being in the presence to God that serves as the primary reason why heaven is a place to look forward to, rather than to be feared. In addition, all three religions depict their conception as a fundamentally peaceful place, where spirits may rest and enjoy perfect harmony. In other words, for almost all religious traditions, the afterlife is the very opposite of our earthly existence and its struggles with greed, envy, hatred, violence, and war.

When we look more closely at the Muslim concept of paradise, the idea of *Jannah* as a Garden of Eden seems to correspond with descriptions by many NDE witnesses during their first encounter with the spiritual universe. The beautiful gardens, the cool streams, and the colorful flowers and trees that populate the

Muslim paradise closely match the near-death experiences that we encountered in Chapter 3. Perhaps it is not inconceivable, then, to suggest that such near-death experiences may actually have inspired some descriptions of paradise in the Hadith. On the other hand, Islam originated as a desert faith, and in that sense *Jannah* is the complete opposite of the desert: it is everything that the Arabian Desert is not. It is a lush oasis filled with date palms, fruits, and sparkling waters.

Where *Jannah* diverges from our concept of heaven is in its emphasis on physical pleasure. As spirits, we will no longer have a physical body that can experience or even crave such things as good food or sex, because having a body also means experiencing all the negative emotions of human life, including pain, anguish, grief and despair. And the whole point of the spiritual universe is to *liberate* us from these feelings, so that we can enjoy and expand our consciousness without any limitation whatsoever.

Of course, we don't do the Muslim faith justice by only focusing on its material aspects. It is undeniably true that imams often emphasize the *spiritual* joy that comes from being in a place with Allah. It is the proximity to the mercy and grace of Allah that offers the believer the greatest source of happiness in paradise. "Allah has promised to believers, men and women, gardens under which rivers flow," says one Hadith, "but the greatest bliss is in the good pleasure of Allah: that is the Supreme Felicity."[130] And some passages stress the fact that the purpose of sexual pleasure in paradise is to allow *everyone* to have this great joy, particularly men and women did not or could not experience conjugal activity during their life on earth.

It is important to see this in the context of traditional Arabic culture. Even today, many young men and women in Arab societies are prevented from having sex until they are married. In order to be married, the young groom has to demonstrate that he has the means to support his future wife and children. With youth unemployment and youth poverty now hovering between 35 and 40% in parts of the Middle East, that means that many Arabs are unable to marry, and are therefore prevented from having sex just when their sexual drive is at its peak.[131]

This explains the deep sexual frustration that runs through many traditional Arab societies, certainly those that are exposed to advertisements, TV shows and social media from the West, where very different morals rule the day. Many scholars believe that the clash between traditional Islamic morals and Western attitudes towards sex and gender was the spark that produced jihadist organizations such as Al Qaeda, ISIS and Boko Haram. This is abetted by extreme imams who claim that those who die as part of the *jihad* against the West—including suicide bombers—are immediately whisked to paradise, where 72 virgins wait to service them. If you are a young man who has watched lots of scantily clad women in American films but has never experienced sex yourself, this can be a powerful incentive. Most Islamic scholars, however, dismiss this nonsense out of hand.

In my book *From Moses to Muhammad*, I trace the jihadist myth of being whisked to paradise to the 1980-1988 war between Saddam Hussein's Iraq and Revolutionary Iran, ruled by the Ayatollah Khomeini. At the time, Khomeini issued a decree that soldiers who gave their life fighting the Iraqis would be considered *shahids*, with free passage to Paradise.[132] To support his claim, Khomeini cited surah 3 from the Qur'an: "Think not of

Baroque depictions of heaven, such as this fresco in Altenburg Abbey, Austria, envisioned a heavenly abode filled with fully clothed human beings, attended by winged angels and *putti*.

those who are slain in Allah's way as dead. Nay, they live, finding their sustenance in the presence of their Lord; They rejoice in the bounty provided by Allah" (Qur'an 3:169).

Khomeini's edict has been used by extremist imams ever since to justify the use of suicide bombers in attacks on Western soldiers and civilians in the Middle East, or acts of terrorism against innocent people throughout the world. These imams, however, ignore the fact that suicide is expressly forbidden in the Qur'an. Sura 4, *An-Nisaa* ('The Women') warns the believers "not (to) kill yourselves, surely God is most Merciful to you" (Q 4:29). According to one Hadith, Muhammad himself said it even more clearly: "He who commits suicide with something, will be punished with the same thing in Hell."[133]

Having said that, for the truly faithful paradise will indeed be a realm filled with physical pleasure. One Hadith even claims that every man in paradise will be given "two wives with transparent skins," and that "nobody will be left unmarried," thus highlighting the idea that every pious Muslim will be rewarded.[134] It is by extending life's greatest joy to every man and woman in paradise that Islam aims to erase the suffering and inequalities that inevitably attended humankind on earth.

Nirvana and Reincarnation

Thoughts about the afterlife have also occupied Asian civilizations from a very early age. From about 1000 B.C. onwards (roughly contemporary with the stirrings of Judaism), Indo-Aryan people in northwestern India produced a series of texts known as the *Vedas* that form the foundational epics of Hinduism, which we have cited throughout this book. Much of the Vedas is concerned with what happens to the soul after death. Scholars believe that in the beginning, these Vedic sages used a variety of hallucinogens to induce altered states of consciousness, so as to unlock their inner spirit. Eventually, they developed other techniques to explore their inner consciousness, including the technique we now know as yoga. This is why ancient India probably became the first culture to recognize that our consciousness is transcendental, and potentially immortal.

Over time, this led Indian sages to the idea that our consciousness can only reach total happiness if every form of material craving is utterly quenched or "snuffed out," like the flame of a candle. This is captured in the word *nirvana,* which literally means "quenching." Nirvana has served ever since as the ultimate goal of Hinduism as well as Buddhism, Jainism, and Sikhism. For these traditions, nirvana is a state of a profound spiritual peace, quiet, and freedom from want. But how followers can attain this nirvana is a point of contention between these traditions.

Buddhism interprets nirvana as the culmination of a long cycle of birth, death and rebirth known as *Saṃsāra* (Sanskrit for "wandering"). In this view, humans are condemned to experience an endless cycle of reincarnation, with the soul aimlessly "wandering" through the universe until through progressive enlightenment it finds ultimate release, known as *moksha.* Seen in this context, Buddhism sees the cycle of life through the prism of inevitable human suffering, and nirvana as an ultimate resolution of that process. The believer achieves that state by reaching ever greater stages of enlightenment, ultimately leading to complete self-denial.

Hinduism, by contrast, sees this process a bit differently. For

Hindus, *Saṃsāra* is above all the journey of the soul, known as *Atman*, and the self, known as *Brahman*. Even though the body changes as it moves through various reincarnations, the soul always remains pure, provided it allows itself to be guided by Hindu gods who help humans to gain self-perfection. It is this state of knowing one's soul, and having achieved perfect harmony with that soul, that constitutes *moksha* – a place "where there is no old age nor death, no pain nor disease." As part of that journey, Hindus seek solace in the guidance of priests as well as a variety of ceremonial rituals that are all absent in Buddhism.

When we compare the concept of nirvana to our spiritual universe, some similarities are immediately apparent. Nirvana constitutes a state of complete spiritual perfection and harmony, which is certainly true for the spiritual universe as well. In both domains, all forms of suffering are banned forever. By the same token, we are relieved of any form of material attachment, which is precisely the goal of Buddhist practice.

Where things get complicated is with the process that believers must accomplish in order to attain the state of *nirvana*. Both Hinduism and Buddhism prescribe a long process of meritorious advancement—one through enlightenment, the other through prayerful good deeds—before the spirit can gain access to its ultimate release. Our spiritual universe, by contrast, does not recognize such a lengthy qualification period, though as we saw, as spirits we will certainly be asked to reflect on the moral quality of our actions in life.

Both Buddhism and Hinduism operate with a concept that we encountered before, namely, the idea of reincarnation. The *Bhagavad Gita*, a major Hindu foundational text, explains that the soul will discard the old body and take on a new one, just as a man may discard his old clothes for new garments. While the body is purely a vehicle to dispose of, the soul itself is indestructible, and as such goes through many different lives in a cycle of birth and death. The quality of the next life, however, is determined by the sum of a person's deeds (or *karma*) in a previous life, as we saw previously. A righteous person may look forward to a new life full of happiness, whereas those who behaved badly may return as a lower creature, such as an animal.

One of the earliest depictions of the Gautama Buddha, dated to the 3rd century A.D., shows the Buddha delivering his first sermon after attaining enlightenment while turning the wheel of dharma, which represents the path to nirvana.

How does this idea of reincarnation relate to our idea of heaven? As we saw, it is true that as spirits, we both originate from and return to that universe once our life is complete. But is that process repeated? Will we as spirits be tasked to go down to the earthly domain as humans once more? Are we programmed to experience this cycle of death and rebirth over and over again, as these Asian religions claim? And if that is true, what would be the point? Why can't we stay in our beautiful home in the spiritual universe, rather than experience the long process of childhood, adulthood and old age all over again?

This is, of course, a very sensitive subject—particularly in a Western context, where Christianity, Judaism and Islam all reject notions of individual reincarnation out of hand. Based on his extensive case studies, Michael Newton also believed that his patients reported going through multiple lives before reaching their current one. There comes a time, he writes, that "souls must prepare to leave a world of total wisdom, where they exist in a blissful state of freedom, for the physical and mental demands of a human body."[135] The purpose, he says, is to atone for past misdeeds or errors in judgment, and with the aid of spirit guides to grow in wisdom and moral understanding. When the soul does return and take human form once more, he writes, all memories of a previous life are erased from its consciousness, though they still persist in the subconsciousness, where they can be excavated by regressive hypnotherapy.

For many of us, this seems like a daunting prospect. Once we make our home in this beautiful spiritual universe and grow close with our spirit family, why would we want to go back? Why would we *need* to go back? What's the point of that?

I think the answer lies in the fundamental difference between the concept of *spirit* and *soul*. I know that our religions often use these terms interchangeably, and that at certain times, this book has done so as well. But the question of reincarnation forces us to make a sharper distinction.

The Spirit and the Soul

As we saw, the spirit is our identity and our consciousness. It is our sense of self, with all the wisdom and experiences we accumulated in life. It is that consciousness that survives the death of our body and returns to the spiritual universe. As such, it will always carry the essential identity that you and I have on earth.

But we also have a soul, and as it turns out, our soul is a very different quantity altogether. Our soul operates at a higher level than our spirit. It is an integral part of the higher domains of the spirit universe, for it serves as the mediator between us and the great living consciousness of the Source. Our soul, in other words, is *our immediate connection to God*.

It is our soul that tasks our spirit to go where it must, to experience human life, and then to return with that experience, so that the soul can absorb and expand the cosmic energy. But to do so, our soul cannot rely on just one spirit "emissary" alone. To fulfill its mission, it can have multiple extensions, just as a tree has many branches. In other words, our soul can issue *multiple spirits*, each charged to live the life of a human being—or perhaps as a different species in other worlds that we don't even know about.

Yes, I know this all sounds a bit strange. To explain this idea, Sue often compares the soul to a flame. "Imagine a flame that is coordinating everything, that it is the god head within you," she says. "That's the divine part—the divine essence of knowing. Now, that flame will cast a light, and that light is our spirit. It goes and travels, like a pod, while the soul stays very close to the Source. And of course, a flame can cast its light in many different directions."

That begins to make some sense. But how does it work? Are we as spirits even *aware* of our spirit siblings? When we "report back" to our soul, can we communicate with other spiritual extensions of our soul? I think that is where the idea of reincarnation comes into play. In other words, while our own consciousness may not have to repeatedly travel back to an earthly existence, we do have spiritual siblings that have a human life of their own. And all of these experiences are ultimately gathered in the central domain of our soul.

This may explain why some people—usually children between the ages of 4 and 9—have memories of an earlier life as a different person. In 1966, Ian Stevenson of the University of Virginia created an uproar when he published the first edition of his landmark book *Twenty Cases Suggestive of Reincarnation*.[136] Stevenson was struck by a particular pattern whereby the "child usually feels a considerable pull back toward the events of a particular life, and he frequently importunes his parents to let him return to the community where he claims that he formerly lived." This may go on for some time, until the parents begin to make inquiries about the accuracy of these recollections.

What is so fascinating about Stevenson's book is that he has even documented cases whereby young children found they could speak a foreign language that no one else in their environment had ever been in contact with (a phenomenon known as "responsive xenoglossy"). While skeptics have offered plenty of reasons why a child can have regressive memories that do not match its own environment, this is one example that cannot be explained away by conventional developmental theory.

But Stevenson drew what I believe is a flawed conclusion from his study, namely, that these children must have had a reincarnation experience *themselves*. For him this was, as he wrote, the "best possible explanation." Actually, the real explanation is more nuanced than that. In my view, the spirit of these children carried information that was not theirs, but experienced by their spirit siblings, and communicated to them through the shared domain of their soul.

This idea does not necessarily negate Buddhist and Hindu teachings. The desire to purify one's spiritual dimension at the expense of one's material gratification is unquestionably an important process towards enlightenment, in this world and the next. The difference is that this cycle does not need to be the *linear* reincarnation cycle that these Asian traditions have posited. It is not our individual spirit that is tasked to relive this cycle over and over again; it is our soul, by virtue of its untold number of permutations.

To better illustrate the role of the soul in relationship to the spirit, Sue likes to tell the story of what a spirit guide once told her. "He said, imagine that you are holding a black card with little pinpricks in front of a candle. We can't see the candle, but we can see the light as it pierces the tiny holes we've punched into the card. Each of those pinpricks is a spirit manifestation of our soul. That means that at any given time, there can be multiple spirits carrying the light of our soul into the universe. And ultimately, all these spirits will return to the soul with the experience they have gathered."

Could this really be true? Is the spiritual universe *that* intelligent? But why would it not be? As we saw before, we only have to look at the pictures of the Hubble telescope to see galaxies of a size and power that simply boggle the mind. If there is a Source that can produce such incredibly complex systems, why would we think that it could not develop equally sophisticated systems in a spiritual sense? And if that is true, then there is no reason why the spiritual domain could not have the same cycle of birth, death and rebirth that we saw in the awesome picture of the Eagle Nebula, as manifested by the various spirits of our soul.

Heaven and the Spiritual Realm

As we saw, the Christian idea of heaven is not as specific as Muslim, Buddhist or Hindu concepts of the afterlife, though its role as the redemptive agency of Christian faith is paramount. Without ideas such as the immortality of the soul and the belief in the reward of heaven, Christianity would not exist. But Christian authors have long resisted the idea of describing heaven as a particular location, in the way that Islamic authors have. As Paul wrote in his first letter to the Corinthians, quoting Isaiah, "eye has not seen, ear not heard, nor the human heart conceived, what God has prepared for those who love him" (1 Corinthians 2:9, quoting Isaiah 64:3).

That has not stopped other authors from trying to imagine what heaven may look like. Several fall back on the idea of a primordial Garden of Eden, as the Qur'an and the Hadith do.

This may be the reason why many NDE patients who experienced visions of a beautiful Shangri-La inevitably associate that memory with the idea of heaven.

What sets the Christian idea of heaven apart is that it is a fundamentally *spiritual* domain, in close proximity to God. There are no material pleasures or distractions of any kind; instead, we are free to experience joy in the company of others—that is, other spirits like ourselves. This is an important distinction, because unlike most Asian religions that emphasize *individual* enlightenment, Christianity is a much more *social* belief system. Throughout the Gospels, Jesus stresses the importance of experiencing things together, whether by coming together on a mountain for a sermon; sharing a meal of bread and fish; or caring for those who are hungry, lame or sick. This is a unique quality of the Christian tradition that stood in sharp contrast to the prevailing worship of Jesus' time; Romans, Greeks, and to some extent even ancient Jews went to the Temple for *private* sacrifice and worship.

By contrast, Christian traditions early on developed the idea of a *eucharistia*, a Greek word that means "thanksgiving." As part of this celebration, early Christians would gather in the home of a believer to sing hymns together, and break bread in imitation of Christ's Last Supper. They would also go out and do charitable works, such as clothing the poor or burying the indigent. This earned them the begrudging respect of many Romans, even though Christianity was not yet an officially tolerated religion. It also meant that when Christianity became fully licensed in the early 4th century with the right to build houses of worship, it didn't have much use for the Roman archetype of a temple. Instead, its architects fell back on another building type, the *basilica*—previously used for civic assemblies—to accommodate large congregations who wished to attend the Christian Mass.

As we saw in the previous chapter, this social aspect is also an important part of the spiritual universe, whereby we as spirits can freely engage with any other spirit regardless of age, distance, or language.

Heaven is for All

When we look at all the evidence that this book has brought together, then the inevitable conclusion must be that heaven is for all. Heaven is where we came from, and to heaven we shall return, as a seamless continuation of our presence as eternal spirit beings.

This does not mean, however, that the moral quality of our actions in life is of no consequence. On the contrary. As we saw previously, as spirits we will be challenged to reflect on what we did, or what we failed to. As a young Spanish patient put it after her near-death experience, "I realized I had wasted time in suffering, and what I should have been doing was using my freedom to choose true love, and not pain, in all that came into my life." That is precisely what the spirit world wants us to do. Not to suffer punishment as a result of our mistakes, but to *learn from them*, and help others on earth to do the same.

The Role of Love

I cannot close this brief comparison between our spiritual universe and religious afterlife concepts without addressing what I think is the most amazing result of our investigation: that the most pervasive element of the spiritual universe is love. "I was filled with love and joy that I cannot describe," an NDE patient named David remembered. Similarly, a patient called Marina said that she no longer had any memory of what it was like to be human; instead, "I just felt love and ecstasy." Or in the words of George, "the love was so good and had answers to everything that I had no questions to wonder about. The happiness I felt was total." And he added, "To have gotten to know this love is the greatest gift I have had in my life."

We know why love is the guiding unit of heaven. The aim of both the physical and spiritual universe is to be cohesive—and love is simply the most powerful energy form that can accomplish that. Time and again, Jesus argued that the Kingdom of God on earth cannot succeed without love as its unifying quality. It is certainly true that in articulating this program, Jesus found inspiration in the prophets of Hebrew Scripture. In Matthew, he cites Hosea when he says, "Go and learn what this means: 'I desire mercy and not sacrifice'" (Matthew 9:13; Hosea 6:6). And Jeremiah, the prophet whom Jesus quotes while chasing the moneychangers from the Temple, taught that "I have loved you with an everlasting love; therefore I have continued my faithfulness to you" (Jeremiah 31:3).

Moreover, I find it fascinating that for both Judaism and Islam, God's most important attribute is mercy, and that the word itself—*rachman*—is virtually the same in both Hebrew and Arabic. The Jewish *Shema V'ahavta*, a profession of faith taken from Deuteronomy, reads "You shall love the Lord your God with all your heart, and with all your soul, and with all your strength, and with all your mind" (Deut 6:5).

But no one urged us more to love than Jesus. For him, love is the paramount virtue of the human condition; it lies at the very core of what it means to be a follower of Christ. When a scribe once asked him which of the commandments is the greatest, Jesus combined the *Shema* with Leviticus: "you shall love the Lord your God .... (and) you shall love your neighbor as yourself" (Mk 12:28-31). The story of the Good Samaritan in the Gospel of Luke is a striking example of what Jesus is talking about (Luke 10:30-37). Selfless, compassionate love as captured in the Greek word *agapè* is what sets Christianity apart from other traditions, no matter how ancient or noble they may be—and that is also carried through in Jesus' vision of heaven.

I realize that I am biased. I was raised a Christian, and have spent much of my career as a scholar investigating the historical context of the man known as *Yeshua*, whom we call Jesus. But while reflecting on the experiences of all the people we have met in these pages, I cannot escape the idea that the love they are talking about is exactly what Jesus had in mind. And that, to me, is powerful evidence for the spiritual universe as described in this book.

The star cluster known as Pismis 24, located in the core of nebula NGC 6357, contains some of the youngest stars in the universe.

8. Living Without Fear of Death

Death is the hardest thing from the outside.
But once inside you taste such completeness, such
peace and fulfillment that you don't want to return.
CARL JUNG, LETTERS, VOL. 1

FOUR YEARS AGO, on a cold February night, I flew back to Holland to bury my mother. It was a Thursday, and ironically, Cathie and I had just returned to Los Angeles after spending the weekend with her in her retirement home near Boxmeer, in the south of Holland. She was in excellent spirits that weekend, even though dementia was slowly eating away at her stamina and her cognitive ability. But she still recognized me, and didn't hesitate when we finally got up from the table and said our goodbyes. She gripped my arm as tears sprang into her eyes.

"Goodbye, darling," she said.

"I will see you in a few months, when we come back," I told her.

"I don't think so," she said, "I might not be around anymore," but she always said that at the end of a visit. It was part of our routine.

"Yeah, right," I said, following the script, "you'll still be here, don't you worry."

She looked into my eyes and said, "No darling, not this time."

Back in Santa Monica, a few days later, my wife was still unpacking our suitcases when the telephone rang. It was my sister Eugenie. "This is the call you have been dreading," she said. That same night, I was on a plane, flying back to Europe.

Later, we all agreed that our visit to Holland was the catalyst for my Mom to finally let go. She had lived a good life, but she always said that she missed me terribly. Of all her children, I was the only one who, some 40 years ago, had chosen to leave the country and finish my degree in the United States, more than 5,000 miles away. Cathie and I always made a point of visiting her at least once a year, and our Sunday morning telephone call to her home was a sacrosanct feature of our lives. But that didn't change the fact that at 93, she was declining at a rapid rate.

You tell yourself that you are prepared for the moment when your parents pass away. It certainly seemed that way with my father, who died fifteen years ago after a long and painful battle with kidney cancer. His death came as a release to him, and that knowledge comforted us as we bore him to his grave. No doubt, I thought, it would be the same with my mother.

And so I buried myself in the logistics of planning the funeral with my brother and sisters, while coping with the stress of trying to organize an event for more than a 100 guests in the span of mere days. But nothing prepared me for the moment when, after the funeral service, the attendants arrived to take my mother's coffin to be cremated. To my surprise, I found my knees buckling under me and I collapsed on a chair, weeping like a child.

Why does the death of a loved one affect us so much? Is it because we fear death? Is it because our minds cannot imagine that the bright spirit that was my mother can somehow escape her frail old body?

I remember sobbing in my chair, staring at her coffin, as my sisters crowded around to comfort me. Why does death hit us so hard? I asked myself. Is it because we feel powerless? Is it because we cannot accept what our religious traditions keep telling us, that some part of us lives on? I took a small wax candle that had burned throughout the service and put it in my briefcase to remind me of a firm resolution: that no matter how long it took, this question was going to be the subject of my new book.

Today, four years later, I know what happened to my Mom when she passed away in her bed at 11:00am. I know that rather than falling into the darkness of oblivion, she found herself released from all her pain, her infirmities and her dementia. Filled with a new sense of purpose, clothed in the glow of a beautiful new spirit, she was led to a gate full of light where her brothers and sisters were waiting for her, to help her cross the threshold of death. And once in the light, I'm sure she was thrilled to see a world filled with the most beautiful orchids and flowers, because painting flowers was the passion of her life.

In the beginning of this book, I wondered how different our world would be if we could only accept that heaven is a natural extension of our human biology. Would we fight as tenaciously to delay a patient's death, even at the cost of great suffering and expense, if we knew the tremendous joy that awaits a person at the other side? And if we did, would we decide to live our lives differently? Would knowing the secret of heaven inspire us to become better human beings?

As part of the research for this book, I asked two of my doctoral students, Jennifer Decker and Michelle Elias, to make a study of whether a near-death experience can fundamentally change a person's life. How does the knowledge of heaven affect us as men and women?

What their research found is that there consistent "aftereffects" from a near-death experience, once the patient is resuscitated and returned to health. The most important result, they found, is that these patients *have lost their fear of death*. Knowing that the afterlife not only exists but actually presents a new beginning, a sense of "homecoming" as many described it, has fundamentally altered their perspective on the end of life. Many of these patients, says Decker, came back with the conviction that the earth is not their real home. "I was conscious of the fact that nothing that I was experiencing (in heaven) was totally new," one patient named Andy said; "the experience brought back memories of a home coming after being away for a long, long, long time."[137]

Another frequently cited effect is that people suddenly grasp the purpose and organization of the universe, and the idea that everyone and everything is connected to the same source of energy. That is why most of these patients experience a fundamental change of behavior after an NDE. Many report feeling a greater sense compassion, of being less judgmental, of having a desire to be of service to others. Many also profess to have a greater interest in spirituality, and feel less attached to material possessions or social status. They no longer crave to have a luxury SUV in their driveway, or to fret about the up and downs of the stock market.

In 1988, Phyllis Atwater published an in-depth study of these behavioral changes in a book called *Coming Back to Life: The After-Effects of the Near-Death Experience*.[138] Atwater, who had no less than three near-death experiences herself, wanted to find out if the emotions she struggled with were shared by other NDE people. Her book confirmed what other studies had shown before: that after an NDE, people tend to become more unconditionally loving, more spiritual, and more peaceful. They also care less for material wealth while wanting to be more of service to others. "I used to get all fired up on political issues," said one of Atwater's witnesses, a man named John, "but they don't seem to be so important now... I can't seem to get myself irate or fuming angry about things not being done as promised, like the car not being ready at the garage, the plumber not showing up on time, or the repairman not keeping his word. They just don't seem to be that important to me anymore."[139]

But she also explored the flip side of a near-death experience, when, as she put it, "known worlds collapse and belief systems collide." What happens when people who have seen "a perfect world and a greater reality" suddenly find that they have to cope with the pressures of human life once more? This shock can be particularly acute if patients find themselves resuscitated in an infirm body that they thought they had left behind. "Waking up" after a near-death experience can also be traumatizing if a patient's social circle of family and friends has difficulty believing what he or she experienced, or accepting the new person that the patient has become. A man named Joe explained, "I believe that it is more difficult for those closest to me, my wife and children, to respond to me as I am now. They will acknowledge that I have changed... It took some time after my experience to accept being human again."[140]

In these cases, the return from an NDE to life on earth can

be challenging, precisely because the patient has changed, but the social environment hasn't. As a woman named Peggy put it, "I am simply not able to perform as I did before. I become distracted and get lost in my thoughts. If I take the dictionary down to look up one word, I may lose myself in it for hours. I want to know everything." And she wryly added, "My home used to be the neatest on the block. Now, answering these questions is more important to me than doing the breakfast dishes." A patient named Susan said, "I feel that everyone lives in a fantasy world, and I am the realist outcast." [141]

On the other hand, when these witnesses do find someone who accepts their experience as authentic, the sense of joy can be overwhelming. "I have been told by some people they can feel the love when I am with them," Joe said. "That makes me very happy because I know that I have shared the love, even if it was non-verbal."

Other evidence for the transformative quality of an NDE is the fact that many patients experienced physical changes after they were brought back to life. In one study, 48.6% reported a greater sensitivity to light, while 35.1 % found they were more sensitive to sound. In addition, 58.1% experienced a greater mental awareness or the ability to process more information. Other people reported having clairaudience (hearing sounds inaudible to others), clairvoyance, clairsentience (feeling the emotional state of others), or telepathy (reading the thoughts of others). [142]

To me, what these testimonies prove is the sheer *depth* of what these patients experienced, in a way that can never be explained away as mere dreams or hallucinations. What these people went through was a game changer, something that transformed the very core of their being.

Another powerful aftereffect of an NDE is a renewed sense of faith and spiritual awareness. Surbhi Khamma and Bruce Greyson decided to investigate this phenomenon in a 2014 study with 229 participants.[143] Their sample was divided in an experimental group consisting of NDE patients, and a control group of normal patients. Those who had an NDE reported significantly more daily spiritual experiences than those who didn't, even long after an actual NDE event. In other words, the new inclination towards faith wasn't simply a passing whim, but a response to a deep-felt need.[144]

What is so amazing about these findings is that they are not limited to patients in the West or Judeo-Christian culture alone. In 2010, a group of researchers published the results of interviews with nineteen Muslims in Iran who had a near-death experience. According to Michelle Elias, the after-effects of these NDE's were very similar to those reported in North America and Europe, including the sense that (1) spiritual values are the most important aspect of life, (2) the next world is more beautiful than life on earth, and that (3) there is no reason to fear death in any way.[145]

Of all these results, the one that I think is most striking is that these people no longer fear death. That is a very hard thing to do, because this fear is literally embedded in our human DNA. As a species, we are programmed for survival, which means that our entire being is predicated on the preservation of our life on this planet, and to avoid anything that may endanger that purpose. That is why we have a fight or flight response, as we saw previously, and why the mechanism of natural selection prompts us to try so hard to stay ahead of our rivals, whether in our work life, our personal life, in sports, or any other endeavor. Death is the antithesis of that quest, which is why we think of death as a catastrophic threat that needs to be delayed or avoided at all costs. Put simply, death is inimical to everything that we think is our purpose on earth, and that is why we dread it.

But astonishingly, most NDE patients have banned this most elementary fear from their lives. As a recent study by Natasha Tassel-Matamua and Nicole Lindsay at Massey University has found, one pervasive after-effect of a near-death experience is not only that the patient no longer fears death, but believes that dying is *an essentially benign process*. As the authors conclude, "not even the most advanced and empirically established psychological therapies" have ever produced the same effect, and certainly not among such a large sample of people.[146]

There are even case studies in which people with a near-death experience felt less inclined to mourn the death of a loved one—much to the surprise of their relatives—because they knew that the deceased was going to a beautiful place, and that they would soon be reunited once more.[147]

That is why I believe that these people who live without fear of death are our most convincing evidence that there *is* an afterlife, and that our consciousness will survive to experience that afterlife to the fullest.

So what does that mean for us, for you and me, as we come to the closing pages of this book? It means that we should have the courage to embrace this knowledge as the good news that it is. I don't know about you, but I think that we all could use a bit of good news in these harrowing times, when so much of our world is divided along the fault lines of tribalism, race, gender, and inequality. And for me, the idea that our consciousness will survive to find a new life in a beautiful world, a heaven filled with love and harmony, is the best news I have heard in a long time.

By the same token, it may also move us to reconsider our behavior, and to realize that the way we treat those with whom we live, work, or play truly *matters*. While heaven is not a theme park to which we must earn entry with good deeds, the evidence in this book shows that what we do in this life has consequences for our life in the next. It tells us that we must be prepared to be accountable for our actions, and to be worthy of the love and mercy that awaits us. To know that we will move to a higher level of consciousness is a great and wonderful gift, but we must make sure that we are worthy of it.

The important thing to remember is that we are part of something much, much bigger than we could ever dream of. As the Veda scriptures put it, the higher the level of consciousness we obtain in life, so much higher will be our development in the spiritual realm. What matters is what we do, both in our lifetime as well as in the hereafter. "We must always remember that whatever we do has a ripple effect on other realms," Sue says, "because everything we do is ultimately linked with everything else."

And that is not always easy, because after you finish reading this book, the world around you will not have changed—at least, not on the surface of it. You will still have a rent or a mortgage to pay; you will still have challenges at work to overcome; and you may still have problems in your personal relationships to resolve. But perhaps these obstacles seem a bit less insurmountable now.

Knowing that there is a new life waiting for us beyond the horizon should inspire us to be more patient and compassionate in our daily lives, even with those people who exasperate us the most.

"Life isn't meant to be such a hurdle as we make it," Sue told me. "That's our free will talking, thinking that we should always be in control. But we don't need to be always in control. When things aren't going in alignment with what you want, you have to learn to let go and surrender yourself to what these powerful energy fields can tell you. When you let your spirit guide lead you, you suddenly feel so much synchronicity and so much more at ease. You begin to feel like a whole person, in a way that no material thing could ever do. And actually, the moment you can start to let go and allow these forces to enrich and empower you, a whole new chapter may open up for you.

"I wish I could share that with the whole world," she said; "the tremendous joy that awaits us in the spirit world."

That is why we wrote this book.

Further Reading

Consciousness Studies in Neuroscience and Quantum Physics

Alexander, E. *Living in a Mindful Universe: A Neurosurgeon's Journey into the Heart of Consciousness*. Piatkus: 2017

Atmanspacher, Harald, "Quantum Approaches to Consciousness," in Zalta, E. (Ed.), *The Stanford Encyclopedia of Philosophy*, Summer 2015.

Becker, A. *What is Real? The Unfinished Quest for the Meaning of Quantum Physics*. New York: Basic Books, 2018.

Carter, C., *Science and the Afterlife Experience: Evidence for the Immortality of Consciousness*. Rochester, VT: Inner Traditions, 2012.

Cohen A.P., Rapport N., *Questions of Consciousness*. London: Routledge, 1995.

Goff, Philip, *Consciousness and Fundamental Reality*. Oxford: Oxford University Press, 2017.

Hameroff, Stuart R., Kaszniak, Alfred W. and Scott, Alwyn C., *Towards a Science of Consciousness (II)*. Cambridge, MA: MIT Press, 1998.

Hawking, Stephen, *A Brief History of Time*. New York: Bantam Books, 2017.

Hennig. B, "Cartesian Conscientia", in *British Journal for the History of Philosophy*. 2007, 15: 455–484.

Murphy, G. "Body-Mind Theory as a Factor Guiding Survival Research," in: *Journal of the American Society for Psychical Research*, Vol. 59 (1965); pp. 148-156.

Searle, J., "Consciousness," in Honderich T,. *The Oxford companion to philosophy*. Oxford University Press, 2005.

Soper, H., Comstock, T., Kissinger, R.E. and Drorit Gaines, K., *Understanding the Frontal Lobe of the Brain*: *Fractioning the Prefrontal Lobes and Associated Functions*. Santa Barbara: Fielding University Press, 2017.

Tononi, G. and Koch, C., "Consciousness: here, there and everywhere?" in *Philosophical Transactions of the Royal Society B*; March 30, 2015.

Van Lommel, P, *Consciousness Beyond Life: The Science of the Near-Death Experience*. HarperOne, 2011.

Near-Death Experiences and Regressive Hypnotherapy

Atwater, P. M. (1988). *Coming back to life: The after-effects of the near-death experience*. Dodd Mead.

Atwater, P. M. *Beyond the Light: What Isn't Being Said About Near-Death Experience*. Carol Publishing, 1994.

Alexander, E., *Proof of Heaven: A Neurosurgeon's Journey into the Afterlife*. Simon & Schuster, 2012.

Degler, T. *A farther shore: How near-death and other extraordinary experiences can change ordinary lives*. HarperCollins, 1996.

Fracasso, C., & Friedman, H., Electromagnetic aftereffects of near-death experiences: A preliminary report on a series of studies currently under way. *Journal of Transpersonal Research*, 2012, 4(2), 34-55.

Fracasso, C., Alejasin, S. A., Friedman, H., Young, M. S., "Near-death experiences among a sample of Iranian Muslims," in *Journal of Near-Death Studies*, 2010, 29(1): pp. 265-272.

Gallup Jr., G. and Proctor, W., *Adventures in Immortality: A*

Look Beyond the Threshold of Death. New York: McGraw Hill, 1982.

Greyson, B., & Liester, M. B. (2004). Auditory hallucinations following near-death experiences. *Journal of Humanistic Psychology*, 44(3), 320-336.

Greyson, B., "Posttraumatic stress symptoms following near-death experiences," in Turner, F. J., *Social work diagnosis in contemporary practice*, Oxford University Press, 2004.

Greyson, B. "Near-death experiences and spirituality," in *Zygon*, 2006, 41(2): 393 – 414

Griffith, L. J., "Near-death experiences and psychotherapy," in *Psychiatry* (Edgmont), 2009, 6(10), 35.

Grof, S., & Grof, C. (Eds.), *Spiritual emergency: When personal transformation becomes a crisis*. TarcherPerigee, 1989.

Holden, Janice Miner; Greyson, Bruce; James, Debbie, (Eds). *The Handbook of Near-Death Experiences: Thirty Years of Investigation*. Santa Barbara: Praeger Publishers, 2008.

Holden, J. M. & Loseu, S. "Shedding light on the tunnel and light in near-death experiences: A case study," in *Journal of Near-Death Studies*, 2015: 34(1): 27-43

Howarth, G., "Dismantling the boundaries between life and death," in *Mortality*, 2000: 5(2): pp. 127-138.

Khamma, S. and Greyson, B., "Daily Spiritual Experiences Before and After Near-Death Experiences," in *Psychology of Religion and Spirituality*, 2014, Vol. 6, No. 4, pp. 302-309.

Kinsella, M. "Near-Death Experiences and Networks Spirituality: The Emergence of an Afterlife Movement," in *Journal of the American Academy of Religion*, Volume 85, Issue 1, 1 March 2017, pp. 168–198.

Long, J. and Perry, P., *Evidence of the Afterlife*. HarperOne, 2010.

Morse, M. (1993). *Transformed by the light: The powerful effect of near-death experiences on people's lives*. Ivy Books.

Newton, Michael, Journey of Souls: Case Studies of Life between Lives. Woodbury, MN: Llewellyn Publications, 1994.

Newton, Michael, Destiny of Souls: More Case Studies of Life between Lives. Woodbury, MN: Llewellyn Publications, 2001.

Ring, K., & Rosing, C. J., "The Omega Project: An empirical study of the NDE-prone personality," in *Journal of Near-Death Studies*, 1990: 8(4), 211-239.

Ring, K., & Valarino, E. E., *Lessons from the light: What we can learn from the near-death experience*. Red Wheel/Weiser, 2006.

Sutherland, C., "Psychic phenomena following near-death experiences: An Australian study," in *Journal of Near-Death Studies*, 1989: 8(2), 93-102.

Targ, R., & Katra, J., "The scientific and spiritual implications of psychic abilities," in: *Alternative therapies in health and medicine*, 2001: 7(3), 143-149.

Tassell-Matamua, N. A. & Steadman, K., "Of love and light: A case report of end-of- life experiences," in *Journal of Near-Death Studies*, 2015: 34(1)

Van Lommel, P., Van Wees, R., Meyers, V., & Elfferich, I. (2001). Near-death experience in survivors of cardiac arrest: a prospective study in the Netherlands. *The Lancet*, 358(9298), 2039-2045.

Vardamis, A. A. & Owens, J. E., "Earnest Hemingway and the near-death experience," in *Journal of Medical Humanities*, 1999: 20(3): 203-217.

Waldron, J. L., "The life impact of transcendent experiences with a pronounced quality of" noesis"," in *The Journal of Transpersonal*

Psychology, 1998, 30(2), 103.

Philosophy, Bio-Energy and Metaphysics

Becker, A. *What is Real? The Unfinished Quest for the Meaning of Quantum Physics* (2018). New York: Basic Books.

Burr, H.S., Northrup, F.S.C. The electro-dynamic theory of life. *Quarterly Review of Biology* 10 (1935): 322-333.

Dirkx, J. M., Mezirow, J., & Cranton, P. (2006). Musings and Reflections on the Meaning, Context, and Process of Transformative Learning: A Dialogue Between John M. Dirkx and Jack Mezirow. *Journal of Transformative Education*, 4(2), 123–139.

Doore, Gary (Ed.), *What Survives? Contemporary Explorations of Life after Death.* Los Angeles: Jeremy P. Tarcher, 1990

Haule, J. R. (2011). *Jung in the 21st Century, Volume One: Evolution and Archetype.* New York: Routledge.

Haule, J. R. (2011). *Jung in the 21st Century, Volume Two: Synchronicity and Science.* New York: Routledge.

Kometer, M., Pokorny, T., Seifritz, E., & Volleinweider, F. X. (2015). Psilocybin-induced spiritual experiences and insightfulness are associated with synchronization of neuronal oscillations. *Psychopharmacology*, 232(19), 3663–3676. https://doi.org/10.1007/s00213-015- 4026-7

Kraehenmann, R., Pokorny, D., Vollenweider, L., Preller, K. H., Pokorny, T., Seifritz, E., & Vollenweider, F. X. (2017). Dreamlike effects of LSD on waking imagery in humans depend on serotonin 2A receptor activation. *Psychopharmacology*, 234(13), 2031–2046.

Lund, D., *Persons, Souls and Death: A philosophical Investigation of an Afterlife.* McFarland & Company, 2009.

Mincolla, M. "Tapping into the Subtle Human Energy Field." *Alternative Medicine*, (16), 46–49.

Olson, Bob, *Answers about the Afterlife: A Private Investigator's 15-year Research Unlocks the Mysteries of Life after Death.* Kennebunkport: Building Bridges Press, 2014.

Richards, W. A. (2014). Here and now: Discovering the sacred with entheogens. *Zygon, 49*(3), 652–665.

Richo, D. (2014). *The Power of Grace.* Boston: Shambhala.

Roach, Mary, *Spook: Science Tackles the Afterlife.* New York: Norton & Company, 2005.

Rohan, M.; Parow, A; Stoll, AL; et al. (2004). "Low-Field Magnetic Stimulation in Bipolar Depression Using an MRI-Based Stimulator". *American Journal of Psychiatry.* 161 (1): 93–98

Rubik, Beverly, "The Biofield: Bridge between Mind and the Body," in *Cosmos and History: The Journal of Natural and Social Philosophy,* vol. 11, no. 2, 2015; pp. 83-96.

Shields, D., Fuller, A., Resnicoff, M., Butcher, H. K., & Frisch, N. (2016). "Human Energy Field," in *Journal of Holistic Nursing,* November 23, 2016.

Shupak, Naomi M; Prato, Frank S; Thomas, Alex W., "Human exposure to a specific pulsed magnetic field: effects on thermal sensory and pain thresholds," in *Neuroscience Letters.* 363 (2): 157–162.

Slawinski, J. "Electromagnetic radiation and the afterlife," in *Journal of Near-Death Studies,* 1987: (6)2, pp. 79—94.

Trungpa, C., *The Heart of the Buddha.* (J. Lief, Ed.) Boston: Shambhala, 1991.

Religious Studies

Abd Al-Wahid Dhannun, D. Taha: *Muslim Conquest and Settlement of Northern Africa and Spain;* Exeter Arabic and Islamic Series, 1988

Addison, James T. *Life Beyond Death in the Beliefs of Mankind.* New York: Houghton Mifflin, 1932.

Bertman, Stephen, *Life in Ancient Mesopotamia.* New York: Oxford University Press, 2005.

Bosworth, C.E., *The Islamic Dynasties: A Chronological and Genealogical handbook.* Edinburgh: Edinburgh University Press, 1967

Brown, Brian, *Noah's other son: bridging the gap between the Bible and the Qur'an.* New York: Continuum, 2007

Chancey, Mark A. *Greco-Roman Culture and the Galilee of Jesus.* Cambridge: Cambridge University Press, 2005.

Chilton, Bruce. *Rabbi Jesus.* New York: Image/Doubleday, 2000.

Cline, Eric: *From Eden to Exile: Unraveling Mysteries of the Bible.* Washington, D.C.: National Geographic Society, 2006.

Crossan, John Dominic. *Jesus: A Revolutionary Biography.* New York: HarperCollins Publishers, 1994.

Davies, Jon. *Death, Burial and Rebirth in the Religions of Antiquity.* New York: Routledge, 1999.

Ehrman, Bart. *Jesus: Apocalyptic Prophet of the New Millennium.* New York: Oxford University Press, 1999.

Evans, Craig A. (Ed). *The World of Jesus and the Early Church.* Peabody, MA: Hendrickson Publishers, 2011.

Finkelstein, Israel and Silberman, Neil Asher, *The Bible Unearthed: Archaeology's New Vision of Ancient Israel and The Origin of its Sacred Texts;* New York NY: The Free Press, 2001.

Geisler, N. & MacKenzie, R., *Roman Catholics and Evangelicals: agreements and differences.* Baker Academic, 1995

Heft, James, *Beyond violence: religious sources of social transformation in Judaism, Christianity, and Islam.* New York: Fordham University Press, 2004.

Hitti, Philip K., *History of the Arabs*; New York: Palgrave MacMillan, 2002

Horsley, Richard A. *Galilee: History, Politics, People.* Harrisburg, Pa.: Trinity Press, 1995.

Isbouts, Jean-Pierre, *From Moses to Muhammad: The Shared Origins of Judaism, Christianity and Islam.* Los Angeles: Pantheon, 2003.

Isbouts, Jean-Pierre, *The Biblical World: An Illustrated Atlas.* Washington, D.C.: National Geographic Society, 2007.

Isbouts, Jean-Pierre. *In the Footsteps of Jesus: A Chronicle of his Life and the Origins of Christianity.* Washington, D.C.: National Geographic Society, 2012

Isbouts, Jean-Pierre. *The Story of Christianity from Ancient Rome to Today.* Washington, D.C.: National Geographic Society, 2014.

Johnson, Christopher J., and McGee, Marsha G., *How Different Religions View Death and Afterlife.* Philadelphia: The Charles Press, 1991.

Lings, Martin: *Muhammad: His Life Based on the Earliest Sources;* Vermont: Inner Traditions Society, 1991

Meier, John P. *A Marginal Jew: Rethinking the Historical Jesus.* Vols. 1, 2, and 3. New York: Doubleday, 1994.

Neusner, Jacob, *The Mishnah: A New Translation.* New Haven, CT: Yale University Press, 1988.

Neusner, Jacob. *Judaism When Christianity Began: A Survey of Belief and Practice.* Louisville: John Knox Press, 2002.

Tottoli, Roberto, *Biblical Prophets in the Qur'an and Muslim Literature.* Richmond, UK: Curzon Press, 2002

Stemberger, Günter. *Jewish Contemporaries of Jesus: Pharisees, Sadducees, Essenes.* Minneapolis: Fortress, 1995.

Stevenson, I., *Twenty Cases Suggestive of Reincarnation.* Charlottesville: University of Virginia Press, 1966; revised and updated edition published in 1980

End Notes

Introduction

[1] Lili Tomlin in the CNN Television special The History of Comedy (2018).

[2] David Lorimer, "Science, Death, and Purpose," in Gary Doore (Ed.), What Survives? Contemporary Explorations of Life after Death. Los Angeles: Jeremy P. Tarcher, 1990; p. 103.

[3] Eben Alexander, Proof of Heaven: A Neurosurgeon's Journey into the Afterlife. Simon & Schuster, 2012.

[4] Colin Wilson, "Glimpses of a Wider Reality," in Gary Doore (Ed.), What Survives? p. 16.

1. A Mountain in Bali

[5] They were all amazed, and they kept on asking one another, "What is this? A new teaching--with authority! He commands even the unclean spirits, and they obey him." Mark 1:27.

[6] That evening, at sundown, they brought to him all who were sick or possessed with demons. And the whole city was gathered around the door. Mark 1:32-33.

[7] Abdul-Sâhib Al-'âmeli, The Prophets, Their Lives and Their Stories; p. 16.

[8] A good introduction to the role of biofield energy is provided by M. Mincolla, "Tapping into the Subtle Human Energy Field." Alternative Medicine, (16), 46–49.

[9] A. S. Eddington, "The Internal Constitution of the Stars." The Scientific Monthly Vol. 11, No. 4 (Oct., 1920), pp. 297-303.

[10] Rohan, M.; Parow, A; Stoll, AL; et al. (2004). "Low-Field

Magnetic Stimulation in Bipolar Depression Using an MRI-Based Stimulator". American Journal of Psychiatry. 161 (1): 93–98.

[11] Thomas, A.W; White, K.P; Drost, D.J; Cook, C.M; Prato, F.S (2001). "A comparison of rheumatoid arthritis and fibromyalgia patients and healthy controls exposed to a pulsed (200 µT) magnetic field: effects on normal standing balance". Neuroscience Letters. 309 (1): 17–20.

[12] Shupak, Naomi M; Prato, Frank S; Thomas, Alex W (2004). "Human exposure to a specific pulsed magnetic field: effects on thermal sensory and pain thresholds". Neuroscience Letters. 363 (2): 157–162.

2. The Energy Within Us

[13] Philip Goff, Consciousness and Fundamental Reality. Oxford: Oxford University Press, 2017

[14] See https://aeon.co/essays/cosmopsychism-explains-why-the-universe-is-fine-tuned-for-life

[15] While traditionally associated with Indian Hinduism, the idea of energy channels as the principal conduits of human energy can also be found in the tantric traditions of Buddhism and Jainism.

[16] Udall DeOleo, The Human Energy Field: A Rediscovered Frontier for Human Development. Unpublished doctoral paper, Fielding Graduate University; 2017; pp. 4-7.

[17] Cajete, G., Philosophy of Native Science: Natural Laws of Interdependence. Sante Fe, New Mexico: Clear Light Publishers, 2016; pp. 46-48.

[18] Beverly Rubik, PhD, "The Biofield: Bridge between Mind and the Body," in Cosmos and History: The Journal of Natural and Social Philosophy, vol. 11, no. 2, 2015; pp. 83-96.

[19] Burr, H.S., Northrup, F.S.C. The electro-dynamic theory of life.

Quarterly Review of Biology 10 (1935): 322-333.

[20] Pressman, A.S. Electromagnetic Fields and Life. New York: Plenum Press, 1970; as cited in Rubik, Beverly, The Biofield; p. 87.

[21] Beverly Rubik, David Muehsam and Richard Hammerschlag, "Biofield Science and Healing: History, Terminology, and Concepts, in: Global Advances in Health and Medicine; Nov. 1, 2015, (Suppl): 8-14. Doi: 10.7453/gahmj.2015.038.suppl.

[22] Sedlak, W. A model of a system radiating the biological field and electrostasis (In Polish). Kosmos A2 (1967): 154-159. Inyushin, V.M. Bioplasma: the fifth state of matter? In: White, J, and Krippner, S. (Eds) Future Science. Garden City, NY: Doubleday (1977): 115-120.

[23] Kilner, W. J., The Human Aura. Kessinger Publishing, 2010.

[24] In the 1990's, a researcher at the University of Southern California, Dr. Valerie Hunt, develop the so-called Bioenergy Field Monitoring System (BFMS) that measured the human energy field up to 200KHz. She posited that any interruptions in the field could be associated with illness or disease. That experiment, in essence, confirmed what Chakra and Chigong practitioners have been saying for thousands of years: that disease is simply the result of an interruption or stagnation in the flow of life energy throughout body. In 2015, the physicist M. Mincolla confirmed Hunt's findings with an even more sensitive instrument, which indicated that the entire human body generates an ambient biofield of 0.025 volts of direct current per centimeter at 10 hertz.

[25] Udall DeOleo, The Human Energy Field: A Rediscovered Frontier for Human Development. Unpublished doctoral paper, Fielding Graduate University; Spring 2017. The cited article is Shields, D., Fuller, A., Resnicoff, M., Butcher, H. K., & Frisch, N. (2016). "Human Energy Field," in Journal of Holistic Nursing, 0898010116678709.

[26] Milo, R., & Phillips, R. (2016). Cell Biology by Numbers. New

York & UK: Garland Science, Taylor & Francis Group.

[27] Including the division of the nuclei, the respiration of mitochondria, and the electrical activity of the brain. See Barenboim, Domanski, & Turoverov, Luminescence of biopolymers and cells. New York : Plenum Press, 1969.

[28] Burke, Upchurch, Dye and Chyu. (2006). "Acupuncture use in the United States: findings from the National Health Interview Survey. The Journal of Alternative and Complementary Medicine, Sept; 12 (7); pp 639-48.

[29] S. Austin, Z. Ramamonjiarivelo, H. Qu and G. Ellis-Griffith. (2015). "Acupuncture Use in the United States: Who, Where, Why, and at What Price." Health Marketing Quarterly, April 2015.

[30] https://en.wikipedia.org/wiki/Acupuncture

[31] Elizabeth Palermo (Ed.). (2017). "What is Acupuncture?" LiveScience, June 21, 2017. https://www.livescience.com/29494-acupuncture.html

[32] B. Rael Cahn; John Polich (2006). "Meditation states and traits: EEG, ERP, and neuroimaging studies". Psychological Bulletin. American Psychological Association. 132 (2): 180–211.

[33] Roger Walsh & Shauna L. Shapiro (2006). "The meeting of meditative disciplines and western psychology: A mutually enriching dialogue". American Psychologist. American Psychological Association. 61 (3): 227–239.

[34] See, for example, Goyal, M; Singh, S; Sibinga, E. M; Gould, N. F; Rowland-Seymour, A; Sharma, R; Berger, Z; Sleicher, D; Maron, D. D; Shihab, H. M; Ranasinghe, P. D; Linn, S; Saha, S; Bass, E. B; Haythornthwaite, J. A (2014). "Meditation Programs for Psychological Stress and Well-being: A Systematic Review and Meta-analysis" in JAMA Internal Medicine. 174 (3): 357–368. For trials related to addiction, see Chiesa A, "Are mindfulness-based interventions effective for substance use disorders? A systematic review of the evidence." in Substance Use Misuse. (Apr 2014). 49

(5): 492–512.

35 Luberto, Christina M.; Shinday, Nina; Song, Rhayun; Philpotts, Lisa L.; Park, Elyse R.; Fricchione, Gregory L.; Yeh, Gloria Y. (2017). "A Systematic Review and Meta-analysis of the Effects of Meditation on Empathy, Compassion, and Prosocial Behaviors," in: Mindfulness. doi:10.1007/s12671-017-0841-8

36 "The mind business." Financial Times, November 21, 2016.

37 Tang, YY; Lu, Q; Geng, X; Stein, EA; Yang, Y; Posner, MI (2010). "Short-term meditation induces white matter changes in the anterior cingulate". Proceedings of the National Academy of Sciences. 107 (35): 15649–15652.

3. On the Threshold of Life and Death

38 Bruce Greyson, "Near-Death Experiences and Spirituality," in Zygon, 41 (2): 393–414, and Bruce Greyson, "Near-Death Experiences Precipitated by Suicide Attempt," in: Journal of Near Death Studies, 1991, Vol. 9 (3)

39 As cited in Jeffrey Long and Paul Perry, Evidence of the Afterlife. HarperOne, 2010; pp. 83-85.

40 Transcript of a television interview of Raymond Moody by Jeffrey Mishlove on the Intuition Network, http://www.intuition.org/txt/moody.htm, retrieved May 2, 2018.

41 Holden, Janice Miner; Greyson, Bruce; James, Debbie, eds. (Jun 22, 2009). "The Field of Near-Death Studies: Past, Present and Future". The Handbook of Near-Death Experiences: Thirty Years of Investigation. Greenwood Publishing Group. pp. 1–16.

42 Janice Miner Holden, EdD, Bruce Greyson MD, and Debbie James MSN, The Handbook of Near Death Experiences: Thirty Years of Investigation. Santa Barbara: Praeger Publishers, 2008; p. 7.

[43] Jeffrey Long and Paul Perry, Evidence of the Afterlife. HarperOne, 2010, p. 28

[44] See: http://www.nderf.org/Archives/NDERF_NDEs.html, retrieved May 11, 2018

[45] G. Gallup Jr. and W. Proctor, Adventures in Immortality: A Look Beyond the Threshold of Death. New York: McGraw Hill, 1982. As quoted in Jeffrey Long, God and the Afterlife. New York: HarperCollins, 2016; p. 3.

[46] Holden, Janice Miner; Greyson, Bruce; James, Debbie, eds. (Jun 22, 2009). "The Field of Near-Death Studies: Past, Present and Future". The Handbook of Near-Death Experiences: Thirty Years of Investigation.

[47] Jeffrey Long, God and the Afterlife, p.

[48] Near Death Experiences Foundation, 4174: Diana H, NDE 8034, posted July 2, 2016. Retrieved May 14, 2018 from http://www.nderf.org/Archives/exceptional.html

[49] Jeffrey Long, God and the Afterlife, p.

[50] Near Death Experiences Foundation, 3839: Arshan. NDE 16074, posted January 19, 2015. Retrieved May 14, 2018 from http://www.nderf.org/Archives/exceptional.html

[51] Ibid, 4040: David. NDE 6135, posted December 30, 2011. Retrieved May 15, 2018 from http://www.nderf.org/Archives/exceptional.html

[52] Ibid, 4193: Marina. NDE 8059, posted August 2, 2016. Retrieved May 15, 2018 from http://www.nderf.org/Archives/exceptional.

[53] Jeffrey Long, God and the Afterlife, p. 13.

[54] Near Death Experiences Foundation, 180: Bill W. NDE 619, posted October 29, 2003. Retrieved May 16, 2018 from http://www.nderf.org/Archives/exceptional.html

55 Noyes, R.; Kletti, R. (1976). "Depersonalisation in the face of life-threatening danger: an interpretation". Omega. 7: 103–114. doi:10.2190/7qet-2vau-ycdt-tj9r.

56 Paulson, D. S. (1999). The near-death experience: an integration of cultural, spiritual, and physical perspectives. Journal of Near-Death Studies. 18(1) Fall 1999.

57 French, Christopher C. (2005-01-01). "Near-death experiences in cardiac arrest survivors". Progress in Brain Research. 150: 351–367.

58 Margot Grey, Return from Death. London: Arkana Press, 1985; p. 86.

59 Zhi-ying, F & Jian-xun, L. (1992). Near-death experiences among survivors of the 1976 Tangshan earthquake. Journal of Near-Death Studies, 11(1), Fall 1992

60 Barber, Theodore X.; Spanos, Nicholas P.; Chaves, John F. (1974). Hypnotism, imagination, and human potentialities. Pergamon Press.

61 See Cartwright, David E. Schopenhauer: A Biography. Cambridge: Cambridge University Press, 2010; p. 181.

62 Michael Newton, Journey of Souls: Case Studies of Life between Lives. Woodbury, MN: Llewellyn Publications, 2019; p. 2.

63 Ibid., page 7.

4. The Search for Consciousness

64 Michael Newton, Journey of Souls; page 18.

65 Charles T. Tart, "Who Survives? Implications of Modern Consciousness Research," in Gary Doore, Ed., What Survives; pp. 138-9.

[66] David H. Lund, Persons, Souls, and Death; pp. 96-103.

[67] Ibid, p. 149.

[68] Jason P. Lerch at al, "Studying Neuroanatomy using MRI." Nature Neuroscience volume 20, pages 314–326 (2017).

[69] Turner R. (2016) Uses, misuses, new uses and fundamental limitations of magnetic resonance imaging in cognitive science. Philosophical Transactions of the Royal Society B. 371: 20150349.

[70] Stuart R. Hameroff and Alwyn C. Scott, "A Sonoran Afternoon," in Stuart R. Hameroff, Alfred W. Kaszniak and Alwyn C. Scott, Towards a Science of Consciousness (II). Cambridge, MA: MIT Press, 1998; p. 639.

[71] Henry Soper et al., Understanding the Frontal Lobe of the Brain: Fractioning the Prefrontal Lobes and Associated Functions. Santa Barbara: Fielding University Press, 2017; p. 11.

[72] Christophe Morin, Neuromarketing and Ethics. Unpublished doctoral paper, Fielding Graduate University, 2011; p. 1.

[73] Karremans, J. C., Stroebe, W., & Claus, J. (2006). Beyond Vicary's fantasies: The impact of subliminal priming and brand choice. Journal of Experimental Social Psychology, 42, 792-798.

[74] "Cartesian" is simply an inversion of "Descartes."

[75] For example, Giulio Tononi and Christof Koch, "Consciousness: here, there and everywhere?" in Philosophical Transactions of the Royal Society B; March 30, 2015. DOI: 10.1098/rstb.2014.0167

[76] Rick Strassman, DMT: The Spirit Molecule: A Doctor's Revolutionary Research into the Biology of Near-Death and Mystical Experiences. New York, N.Y.: Park Street Press, 2001.

[77] Stuart Hameroff, MD, and Roger Penrose, FRS, "Discovery of quantum vibrations in 'microtubules' corroborates theory of

consciousness," in Physics of Life Reviews, January 16, 2014.

[78] Scientists Found that the Soul Doesn't Die – It Goes Back to the Universe, retrieved on September 4, 2018 from https://wakeupyourmind.net/life/scientists-found-that-the-soul-doesnt-die-it-goes-back-to-the-universe/.

[79] J. Allan Hobson, "The Conscious State Paradigm: A Neuropsychological Analysis of Waking, Sleeping, and Dreaming," in Stuart R. Hameroff, Alfred W. Kaszniak and Alwyn C. Scott, Towards a Science of Consciousness (II); p. 473.

[80] John Williams, "Who Says Religion and Science Don't Mix," in The New York Times, June 26, 2017. The article includes an interview with Jay Lombard about his book The Mind of God. New York, N.Y.: Harmony, 2018.

[81] Bernard d'Espagnat, "Consciousness and the Wigner's friend problem," in Foundations of Physics, 12/2005, Vol. 35, #12.

[82] Adam Becker, What is Real? The Unfinished Quest for the Meaning of Quantum Physics. New York: Basic Books, 2018.

[83] Blackmore, Susan (1984). "A Postal Survey of OBEs and Other Experiences".

5. The Psychic Experience

[84] Brent, S. B. (1979). Deliberately induced, premortem, out-of-body experiences: An experimental and theoretical approach. In B. Kastenbaum (Ed.), Between life and death (pp. 89- 123). New York: Springer.

[85] Gardner Murphy, "Body-Mind Theory as a Factor Guiding Survival Research," in: Journal of the American Society for Psychical Research, Vol. 59 (1965); pp. 148-156.

[86] See D. Cliff, "Computational Neuroethology: A provisional manifesto," in J.-A. Meyer and S. W. Wilson (editors): From

Animals to Animats: Proceedings of the First International Conference on the Simulation of Adaptive Behaviour (SAB90). MIT Press Bradford Books, 1991, pp. 29–39.

[87] Maryan Mott, "Did Animals Sense Tsunami was Coming?" in National Geographic News, January 4, 2005.

[88] http://caps.ucsf.edu/wordpress/wp-content/uploads/2011/02/bem2011.pdf

[89] Britt, R.: "Higher Education Fuels Stronger Belief in Ghosts." LiveScience, January 2006, Retrieved September 18, 2007.

[90] David W. Moore (June 16, 2005). "Three in Four Americans Believe in Paranormal". Gallup News Service. Retrieved 2008-10-08.

[91] See https://www.cbsnews.com/news/poll-most-believe-in-psychic-phenomena/, retrieved June 19, 2018.

[92] McConnell, R.A., and Clark, T.K. (1991). "National Academy of Sciences' Opinion on Parapsychology," in Journal of the American Society for Psychical Research, 85, 333–365

[93] Charles T. Tart, "What Survives? Implications of Modern Consciousness Research," in Gary Doore (Ed.), What Survives? pp. 140-141.

[94] Documents concerning the Life and Character of Emanuel Swedenborg Collected, Translated and Annotated by Tafel, RL. Volume II, Part 1. (Swedenborg Society, British and Foreign. 36 Bloomsbury Street, London, 1877).

[95] Karl Christian Wolfart, Mesmerismus oder System der Wechselwirkungen. Theorie und Anwendung des thierischen Magnetismus ("Mesmerism or the system of inter-relations. Theory and applications of animal magnetism"), 1814.

[96] The patient was a highly talented 18-year old musician named Maria Theresia von Paradis, who became blind at an early age.

Some believe that Mozart's Piano Concerto No. 18 was written for her.

97 The work of the commission faltered when the suggestion arose that perhaps Mesmer had discovered a secret physical fluid, which was of course not at all what the German physician claimed. As a result, the committee's findings were not in Mesmer's favor, and the German had little choice but to pack his bags and move to Switzerland. Four years later, the French Revolution toppled Louis XVI and condemned him to the guillotine.

98 Rick Atkinson, The Guns at Last Light. Little, Brown, 2013; pp. 408-409.

99 For more about Cayce's readings, visit https://www.edgarcayce.org.

100 Sugrue, Thomas (1942). There Is a River. Virginia Beach, VA: A.R.E. Press (2003, 50th Anniversary edition), pp. 356–7.

101 Eben Alexander, Living in a Mindful Universe: A Neurosurgeon's Journey into the Heart of Consciousness. Piatkus: 2017.

6. A Journey Through the Afterlife

102 Slawinski, J. (1987, Dec.) Electromagnetic radiation and the afterlife. Journal of Near-Death Studies. (6)2, pp. 79—94.

103 P. M. H. Atwater, Beyond the Light: What Isn't Being Said About Near-Death Experience. Carol Publishing, 1994.

104 NDERF, Randi S, dated April 24, 2004. NDE 952.

105 The man responsible for these amazing visions was an Argentinian artist and production designer named Eugenio Zanetti. He was duly rewarded for his magnificent design with an Academy Award. As it happened, our paths crossed in 2017, when Eugenio appeared in my film The Search of the Last Supper, and I spent an evening at the Sofitel in Hollywood, interrogating him

on how he produced these amazing effects. As it happens, Zanetti is a revered artist in his native Argentina.

[106] Michael Newton, Journey of Souls; p. 24.

[107] Atwater, Beyond the Light.

[108] Source: NDERF: http://www.nderf.org/Archives/2_6_2017.html; retrieved July 3, 2018.

[109] Jean-Pierre Isbouts, The Story of Christianity. Washington, D.C.: National Geographic, 2014.

[110] Source: NDERF: http://www.nderf.org/Archives/2_6_2017.html; retrieved July 3, 2018. NDE 8417.

[111] Michael Newton, Journey of Souls; p. 107.

[112] NDERF, NDE 8250.

[113] Michael Newton, Journey of Souls; p. 51.

[114] Ibid., STE 8347.

[115] Speyer, Erzählungen, pp 61-73

7. The Spiritual Universe and Our Religious Beliefs

[116] Abdul-Sâhib Al-'âmeli, The Prophets, Their Lives and Their Stories; p. 28

[117] Al-Tirmidhi, Sunan. Vol. IV: "The Features of Heaven as described by the Messenger of Allah." Chap. 21. Hadith: 2687, and also quoted by Ibn Kathir in his Tafsir (Qur'anic Commentary) of Surah Rahman (55), ayah (verse) 72.

[118] Shamaa-il Tirmidhi, Chapter 035, Hadith Number 006 (230).

[119] "And whoever desires other than Islam as religion—never will

it be accepted from him, and he, in the Hereafter, will be among the losers." Quran 3:58

[120] The full citation reads: ""But your dead will live; their bodies will rise. You, who dwell in the dust, wake up and shout for joy. Your dew is like the dew of the morning; the earth will give birth to her dead." Isaiah 26:19.

[121] The full citation reads: "People, despite their wealth, do not endure; they are like the beasts that perish. This is the fate of those who trust in themselves, and of their followers, who approve their sayings. They are like sheep and are destined to die; death will be their shepherd (but the upright will prevail over them in the morning). Their forms will decay in the grave, far from their princely mansions. But God will redeem me from the realm of the dead; he will surely take me to himself." Psalms 49:12-15.

[122] Virgil, Aeneid; 6.641.

[123] Homer, Odyssey; 4:560–565.

[124] Dante, Divina Commedia; Par Canto XV Line 25–27.

[125] See, for example, Rabbi Evan Moffic, "Do Jews Believe in an Afterlife?" on ReformJudaism.org; May 10, 2012. I had the great pleasure of interviewing Prof. Levine about this and other topics in 2003 for my book From Moses to Muhammad.

[126] John 14:2

[127] The sympathy that some Pharisees may have felt towards Jesus' ministry is attested in other Gospel stories as well. Luke, for example, tells us that when Jesus "went through one town and village after another," he was approached by "some Pharisees." They had come to warn him that Herod Antipas was aware of his growing following. "Get away from here," these Pharisees urged, "for Herod wants to kill you" (Luke 13:31). This story directly contradicts Mark's theory that the Pharisees and Herod were in collusion to kill Jesus. Indeed, shortly after this episode, Jesus sits down for dinner with "a leader of the Pharisees" (Luke 14:1).

Much later, it is Gamaliel, a noted Pharisaic sage, who defends Peter and other Apostles during their hearing in front of the Sanhedrin (Acts 5:59).

[128] Elisabeth Schussler Fiorenza, In Memory of Her: A Feminist Theological Reconstruction of Christian Origins. London: SCM Press, 1983; p. 100.

[129] See Norman Geisler & Ralph MacKenzie, Roman Catholics and Evangelicals: agreements and differences. Baker Academic, 1995; p. 143.

[130] at-Tawbah 9/72

[131] Source: International Labour Organization, August 24, 2016. The ILO's World Employment and Social Outlook 2016, "Trends for Youth" report shows that the global number of unemployed youth is set to rise by half a million this year to reach 71 million (table 1) – the first such increase in 3 years. Of particular concern is the share and number of young people, often in emerging and developing countries, who live in extreme or moderate poverty despite having a job. In fact, 156 million or 37.7 per cent of working youth are in extreme or moderate poverty (compared to 26 per cent of working adults).

[132] The theological basis for Khomeini's finding was that Saddam Hussein was a tyrant, and that therefore soldiers who died fighting this tyrant were akin to the great Shi'ite martyr Husayn ibn 'Ali, who died fighting the "tyranny" of the Ummayad caliph Yazid. See Jean-Pierre Isbouts, From Moses to Muhammad: The Shared Origins of Judaism, Christianity and Islam. Los Angeles: Pantheon Press, 2011.

[133] Sahih al-Bukhari, Volume 8, Book 73, number 73 and number 126. This is reinforced in Volume 2, Book 23, Number 445 and Volume 8, Book 78, Number 647 .

[134] Bukhari, Badul-khalq 8; Jannah 14

[135] Michael Newton, Journey of Souls; p. 201.

[136] Ian Stevenson, Twenty Cases Suggestive of Reincarnation. Charlottesville: University of Virginia Press, 1966; revised and updated edition published in 1980.

8. Living Life without Fear of Death

[137] Andy Petro, Death Before Dying: A Love Experience by Andy Petro, retrieved from Vital Signs, issue 25 #1, www.IANDS.org

[138] P. M. H. Atwater, Coming Back to Life: The After-Effects of the Near Death Experience. New York: Dodd, Mead & Co., 1988. Republished by Ballentine Books in 1989, and by Transpersonal Publishing in 2008.

[139] Ibid, p. 94.

[140] Ibid, p. 106.

[141] Ibid, p. 75.

[142] Ring, K., & Rosing, C. J. (1990). The Omega Project: An empirical study of the NDE-prone personality. Journal of Near-Death Studies, 8(4), 211-239.

[143] Surbhi Khamma and Bruce Greyson, "Daily Spiritual Experiences Before and After Near-Death Experiences," in Psychology of Religion and Spirituality, 2014, Vol. 6, No. 4, pp. 302-309.

[144] See also Michael Kinsella, "Near-Death Experiences and Networks Spirituality: The Emergence of an Afterlife Movement," in Journal of the American Academy of Religion, Volume 85, Issue 1, 1 March 2017, Pages 168–198.

[145] Fracasso, C., Alejasin, S. A., Friedman, H., Young, M. S., "Near-death experiences among a sample of Iranian Muslims," in Journal of Near-Death Studies, 2010, 29(1): pp. 265-272.

[146] Natasha Tassell-Matamua, Nicole Lindsay, Simon Bennett, Hukarere Valentine, John Pahina. (2017) Does Learning About Near-Death Experiences Promote Psycho-Spiritual Benefits in Those Who Have Not Had a Near-Death Experience?. Journal of Spirituality in Mental Health 19:2, pages 95-115.

[147] Hermann, E.J. (1990). "The near-death experience and the Taoism of Chuang Tzu." Journal of Near-Death Studies. 8(3) Spring 1990

Printed in Great Britain
by Amazon